Fernand Cuny's

BOXING

A 2018 translation
by
Matthew Lynch

Translator's Note:

For as long as there have been dudes, they have been punching one another in the face. Minoans, Sumerians, Hittites, Assyrians, Greeks and Romans were all known to have made a sport and an art of pugilism, forever refining the techniques of beating one another senseless with fists alone. In Sardinia ancient bronze statues of boxers were found adorning the mysterious Nuragic grave sites. In the Iliad Odysseus partakes in the funeral games of Patroclus and smashes some guy's face in. In Virgil's Aeneid, Dares and Entellus go at it like Ali and Frazier such that "cracks of blows upon the ribs resound/ the flailing fists spare not the ears nor brows" until Dares gets carried off by his corner-men, "...with swollen face and lolling head/ that flops side to side, and misshapen mouth/ from which at times drop blood and teeth..." In 13th century

Russia religious festivals were known to include people punching one another in the skull starting with the kids and working up to the prizefighters. Every Christmas morning the good citizens of Santo Tomas in Peru, instead of opening presents like a bunch of sissies, head to the bullfighting ring to beat the bejeezus out of one another to celebrate the festival of Takanakuy. And what St. Patrick's day is complete without a screening of *The Quiet Man,* wherein John Wayne (as ex-boxer Trooper Thorn) slugs it out with Victor McLaglin for a ridiculously long period time, stopping only for the occasional beverage.

Indeed, boxing is a great sport that seems to go with being human. While you can find 1,001 lessons to enlighten you on the current state of the pugilism, this rather obscure manual by French boxer Fernand Cuny (1880-1937) provides a glimpse of some less familiar techniques as boxing transitioned from the bareknuckle age to the days of 4 to 8 ounce gloves. Some advice provided here is timeless for western boxing, while some other pointers seem to hail more from the world of Muay Thai or other striking arts.

While Cuny's rambling style and occasional repetitiveness suggest that he himself was a bit punchy, he clearly knows his stuff and wants to perpetuate his sport. Whether you take interest in details like a splash of bordeaux as being part of a sporty nutritional regimen, or the fact that you might catch a jab in your open hand backed up to your face, every fan of sporting history should find something of interest in Fernand Cuny's *La Boxe.*

M. Lynch, 2018

Fig. 1.-Closed guard

Fig.2.-Open guard.

NOTE

For many people it would seem that boxing is a difficult art requiring long months of study.

It is a great error to believe this. Nothing could be easier to learn than boxing, and I am sure to astonish when I say that at the end of a month of lessons, a beginner who barely seems to get by at first will be ready to spar in the ring. This is of course only if he adheres to the type of boxing he has learned in this course.

I do not mean to say that this same novice will box like a professional--far from it. But he will be in a position to display competence.

First and foremost, boxing is built on immutable principles which never change regardless of the particular method one employs.

These are precisely the principles I will be expounding in this work.

I did not invent these principles, they are the result of the studies made in the best English and American schools of the sport.

Much is said in France regarding the American and English methods. The classic strikes are executed in an identical fashion with a few insignificant variations added by the more scientifically minded boxers of both nationalities.

Discussions regarding distance, and whether closing or maintaining distance is the better tactic in combat, go on infinitely.

And therein lies the problem, as people are always talking about *fighting* when it is a matter of boxing. We can fight without boxing, but it is better to fight *with* boxing.

This latter choice is better seeing as it is a given fact that, I repeat, *nothing could be easier to learn than boxing.*

One must however learn to box before fighting.

A scientific boxer, from my point of view, is not the one who delivers the most varied blows with more or less vigor, but the one who throws his punches, few as they may be, in a classic fashion and with precision. He does nothing more than what needs to be done at the opportune moment and with the least effort possible.

In England, the cradle of boxing, from the least novice to the man who attends every public match, every man knows the fundamentals of boxing. No error committed by a boxer in the ring escapes the notice of the English public.

This explains why so many French boxers who have fought on the other side of the channel claim to have been the victims of bad decisions rendered by British judges who attach enormous importance to fundamental principles.

This is not the place to discuss the rightness or wrongness of this style of judging. I will only say that in France we see boxing as more of a show than a sport. When I say that the public sees boxing as a show, I do not mean to imply that a horde of people are taking the time to come to boxing matches. Quite to the contrary, not enough people turn out and I am sorry to say we in France are still far from witnessing the kind of turnout seen in America and Australia at the big boxing matches.

But to clarify my thought, I mean that I would like to see that each spectator who shows up at a boxing match does practice or has practiced boxing for a time in a hall or a club under the direction of a competent instructor.

Do not tell me that this idea is utopian.

Everyone can learn to box, rich and poor. For expensive clubs and professors you can find highly capable teachers to give you a course in boxing for 5 to 10 francs a month. Other serious clubs offer instruction for less than two francs a month.

Both the strong and the weak can box making use of their different means.

Let no one say that he has no time for sport.

In the gyms, halls and clubs they box from the earliest hours of the morning to late at night.

It would be one heck of a situation if, in the course of a week, a person could not find and hour or two in the morning, afternoon or evening.

Do not believe those who say that learning to box translates directly into black eyes, a broken nose, a busted jaw or broken ribs.

These are the arguments, and absolutely false ones, of the enemies of the sport.

Such accidents are exceedingly rare and belong mainly to the professionals who fight in public with light 4 ounce gloves which have little padding.

Now the amateur who boxes on a gym with highly padded 8 ounce gloves will not come to harm whether he is working out with his teacher or having a friendly sparring match with a comrade.

So for all of you who are fans of the sport, you have absolutely no excuse not to practice it. For those of you who claim to lack the stamina, you will acquire it. The overweight will slim down, and weak will gain strength, and the slim will beef up.

This sounds like I am selling snake-oil, but it is the absolute truth and I defy anyone to try it and prove me wrong, even if he be completely inept at sports or exercise.

In any case, there should not be an able young man today who has never practiced "the noble art" for at least a few months.

I will not go on about the physical benefits of boxing as physical exercise, as everyone knows them.

From a psychological standpoint boxing is also the most excellent sport.

Aside from a very high degree of development of the faculties of judgement, volition, and dexterity arising from boxing, I have observed that the young people who have given themselves over to the sport have become better people in the broadest sense, and their style of reasoning and their ideas have become much more serious.

The practice of boxing seems to "harden" a person in some sense and we can say that, like travel, boxing has a positive formative influence on our youth.

It teaches us to count only upon ourselves, as well as all of the fine manly qualities: stoutheartedness, stoical courage, energy, and the spirit of chivalry come naturally to the boxer.

———————

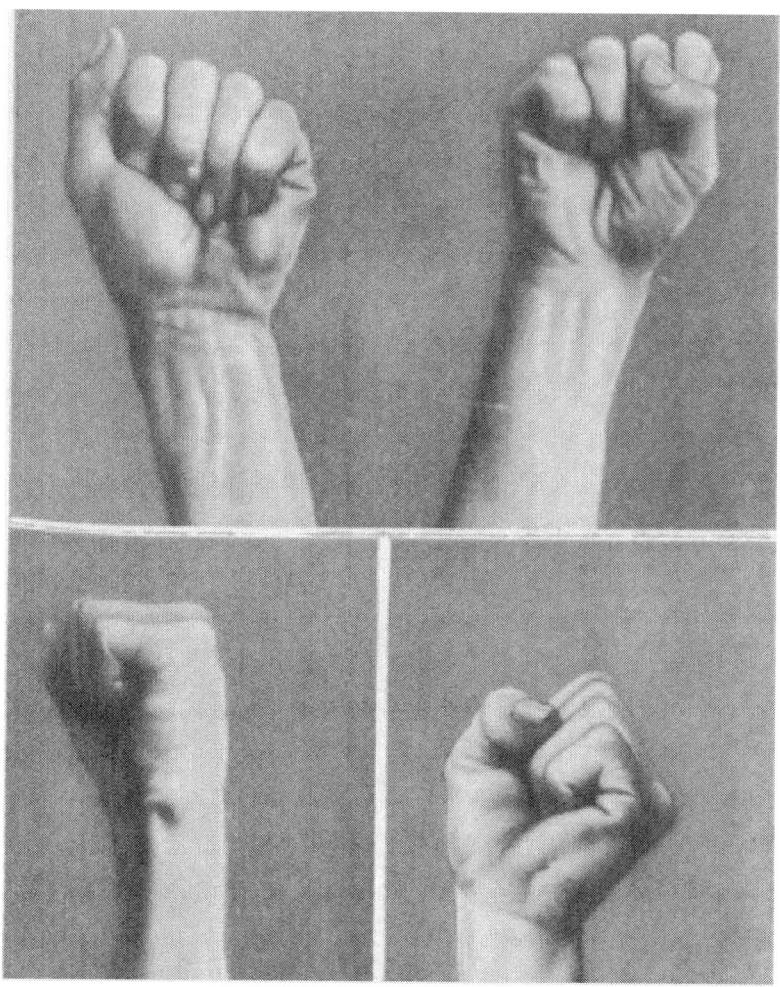

(Top) Fig. 3.-Improper thumb position.-Proper thumb position.
(Bottom left.) Fig. 4. -Proper fist position.
(Bottom right.) Fig. 5. -Improper fist position.
Never bend your wrist.

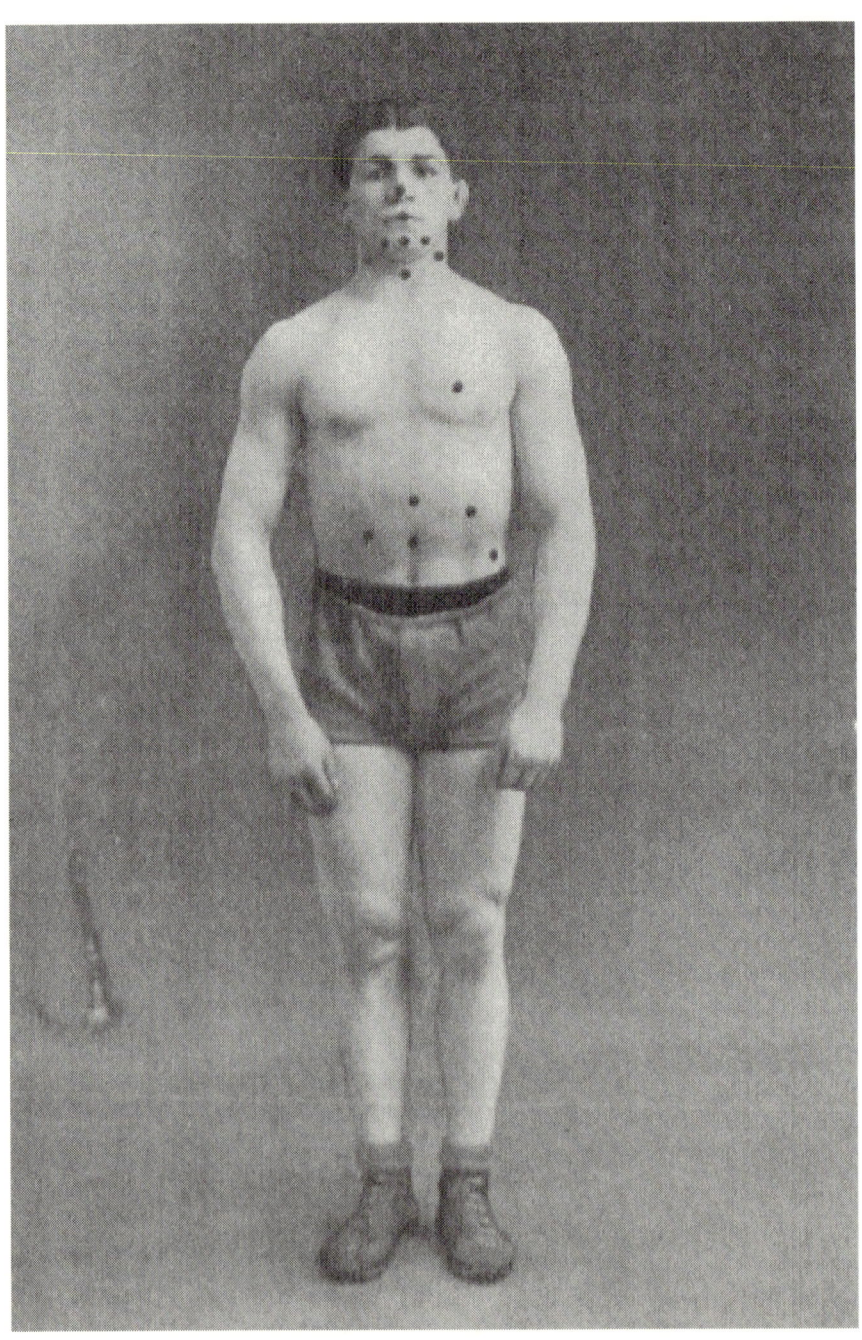
Fig. 6.-The points indicate sensitive areas of the body.

BOXING IN ANTIQUITY

I do not wish for this book to pass beneath the eyes of the reader without him having read a certain curious and erudite study on the origins of the "noble sport of self-defense."

It is in the form of an article written by M. Dalbanne in the sports magazine *Physical Education* featuring documents written by eminent ancient authors, in particular Mercurialis in his "De Arte Gymnastica," a work available to all who are curious at the National Library.

There you can see that the pugilists of ancient times were already employing the same training methods as our modern boxers.

Origins of Boxing

Boxing or more properly speaking pugilism has always existed, and to find its origins we must look to greatest antiquity.

It is clear that the first men would have had recourse, like the animals, to the simplest arms furnished them by nature, which is to say that wrestling and boxing were born at the same time or nearly so.

The ancient Greeks, who never failed to make the best possible use of all bodily exercises, came to love pugilism. They studied and perfected it and finally taught it at the level of all of the other arts. Not only did they use it to prepare for war, but they used it as a form of mass entertainment, and it found its place among the program of events for religious ceremonies and public festivals.

In the earliest centuries of Greek culture we find heroes who staked all of their glory on their power and skill as boxers.

Thus we find that it is to Amycus, king of the Bebryciens who were formerly barbarian and son of Neptune and the nymph Melia, that Plato ascribes the institution of boxing.

Amycus never allowed a foreigner to cross his lands without fighting with him, but he was beaten and killed by Pollux the Argonaut who he had challenged.

Theocritus and Apollonius celebrate this victory and a fable by Photius shows Amycus as the greatest pugilist: "On his tomb a pink laurel grew, and whoever ate of it could not help but love boxing."

Thus the sport found its way into every gymnasium and all of the public games. In the Iliad Homer includes pugilism in the games held on the occasion of the death of Patroclus. In the Odyssey Ulysses attends a boxing match in Scheria. Despite its popularity pugilism did not appear in the Olympic games until the 23rd Olympiad, and according to Pausanias it was Onomastus of Smyrna who gained first prize in boxing.

Finally the art was glorified in sculpture, and antique vases reproduce for our eyes the postures of the combattants and their manner of punching.

In the Southern Metopes of the Parthenon, of which there are castings in the Louvre, we can see that in their battle with the centaurs the Lapiths delivered punches to the jaw and ribs in the same fashion employed today.

It is probable that in the beginning boxing was practiced with bare fists, then fighters wrapped their hands and wrists in a network of thin leather straps held together in the palm of the hand to form a sort of glove.

These gloves were called *himantes* and appeared to have been intended to deaden blows rather than increase their power.

If you look at the paintings adorning a relief from Vulci you can see two boxers tied up together in the presence of a trainer.

The two fighters are wearing *himantes* and the trainer seems to pointing out bad form, all of which seem to indicate that this is a sparring session.

Later, in order to render punches more dangerous, the fighters would replace their soft leather straps with hard leather straps fitted with studs or plates of copper or lead. Such instruments, called *cestus* by the Roman writers, had various names among the Greeks. Homer refers to them as *Imas* and *Myrmex*.

We have produced some sketches of the *cestus* according to the description of Mercurialis. It is easy to see that with such equipment the pugilist was involved in one of the most brutal and dangerous of sports.

The athletes who engaged in this type of boxing were totally disfigured and the enthusiastic poets celebrated them.

In Greek literature we find four epigrams by Lucilius and one by Lucien the most relevant of which depicts a pugilist who became so disfigured that he was unable to collect the money his father had left him in his will. His brother produced an old portrait of him in court, and as this bore no resemblance to the man in question, he was dispossessed.

But the exercises leading up to an actual fight were not undertaken with the most damaging gloves. Here spherical gloves were affixed to the hands with straps allowing the fighter to get a feel for the *cestus* without the heaviness and hardness.

This preparatory exercise was known as *spheromachia*.

But the excessively brutal nature of the blows received in a fight led pugilists to to adopt a sort of helmet which covered the most exposed areas. These *amphotides* covered the head and ears. The metal used for these seems to have been bronze.

———

In the beginning boxing did not seem to have any rules save to strike as hard as possible in order to arrive at the desired result quickly. Later on some athletes made it a science wherein skill and endurance figured heavily.

The boxers best known to historians are certainly Glaucus and Melancomas, the favorite of the emperor Titus.

This latter fighter exhausted his adversaries with his boundless stamina. He was so hardened to work and fatigue that he could "could fight match after match continuously for two consecutive days" (!).

Let us also mention that according to Elien, Eurydamas of Cyrene "had his teeth broken by a punch, but did not let it show. He swallowed his teeth along with the blood from the wound and through this ruse vanquished the opponent who had wounded him without knowing it, and who rarely wavered when he received a punch such that he would win in the end."

We find many descriptions of boxing from the Greeks, the oldest of which comes to us from Homer in the 23rd book of the Iliad. Here we find a boxing match between Epeus, builder of the wooden horse, and Euryale.

Euryale is hit hard and hurled to the ground "his friends surrounding him and lifting him up, his legs dragging, spitting thick blood, his head lolling to the side and his mind absent."

Is this not a scene which often plays out in the course of serious English boxing matches?

Two other Greek poets who were almost contemporaries, Theocritus and Apollonius of Rhodes, described the fight between Pollux the chief of the Argonauts and Amycus, king of the

Bebricians, an encounter that ended in the death of the latter.

Various Roman writers, among them Virgil in his *Aeneid,* also provide detailed descriptions of pugilism.

Among the Greeks the original boxers came from Arcadia, Elide, Egine, and Rhodes.

It was a son of this last city, Diagoras, of whom Pindar sang. After winning many laurels in his youth, the aged Diagoras brought his two sons to the Olympic games and, upon seeing them declared victors, he died in their arms in a transport of joy.

In his work on gymnastics, Philostratus describes the constitution of a fighter in the following terms: "A good fighter must have long arms, a good right, powerful shoulders, and a straight neck. He must have the heaviest hands for striking, that are at the same time big and supple to deal punches easily. The pelvis must be a solid foundation for the athlete, for in throwing his hands to strike, the body will seem weightless unless the hips are involved. As for those with big calf muscles, I don't find them suited for any sport, least of all pugilism. The legs must be straight and symmetrical with space between the thighs, as this gives the most power to athletes. The stomach which does not project too much is advantageous for fighters who draw power and good breathing from it."

We also see ancient pugilists making use of the punching bag or *Corycos* which was much like the modern version, as well as the sandbag.

This exercise had the name of *corymachia* and Philostratus, Plato, Oribasius, and Mercurialis speak of it in a fashion that is sufficiently clear.

It was a leather sack suspended from the ceiling of the gym, and here is what Oribasius says of it: "For novices the sac is filled with grain or flour, and for those who are accustomed to it it is filled with sand. The size must be in proportion to the strength and age of the athlete. It is suspended in such a way that the bottom of the bag comes to the belt-line. The athlete will take it and give it a push, first lightly and by degrees more powerfully, then allows it to swing on its own, meeting it

(Fig. 7.[left]-Exchanging punches.)

with his fists and at times his chest to get used to the shock. This exercise fortifies the muscles, the shoulders, and the entire body. Such were the customs of the pugilist of yore to train for a sport that was harsher and more brutal than the modern boxing to which it gave rise.

(Fig. 8.[Left]-Direct left to the face or *jab* and a block.)

Nothing resembles ancient boxing more than its modern counterpart in English boxing. Boxing is known to have made its first appearance on the first ages of British history but the rules governing it date only from the 18th century, when the famous Jack Broughton had the pugilistic world adopt them around 1743.

It is curious to note that, just as in Greece, boxing had two successive schools. In the first, power and toughness alone came into play as the two combattants stop opposite one another and hammered one another conscientiously while hardly moving.

The second school made use of skill and science, great mobility and the art of dodging blows.

And indeed it is true that there is nothing new under the sun, that nothing disappears and everything is renewed. Following the example of antiquity the famous boxer Peter Jackson, known as the "black anvil", shall have his statue erected in Sydney's Centennial Park.

We say "shall" because from what we know of the Director of the *Sydney Referee* who made the proposal, we take for granted that the project will be approved.

THE GUARD.

When two opponents face off in a sparring session or a match in English boxing they will, at the given signal, advance and shake hands. This occurs at the beginning of the first round and after the last.

Immediately after this the fighters assume the guard position.

We assume the guard position by placing the left foot and the shoulder forward and the right foot and shoulder back.

The feet must be suitably wide apart (40 to 60 cm) so as to insure a solid equilibrium that allows us to absorb blows, but not so far apart as to hamper mobility.

You should keep the weight not on the toes, which would be tiring, but on the front of the feet such that the heel touches the floor without resting upon it.

The legs are placed almost on the same line perpendicular to the opponent (see figures 1 and 2).

The arms and fists should be held in the following way:

The left arm is bent so that the elbow is placed in front of the stomach with the hand open and the palm out at the height of or rather beside the chin to the left (see figures 1 and 2).

I insist particularly upon this point because I have seen many boxers assume the wrong defensive posture putting the hand to the right side of the face such that it is easy for the opponent to connect with a straight left.

The arms must not be tense. You must leave the muscles loose to obtain a speed which should always be natural and not forced. It should be proportional to the speed of the opponent since in boxing the moral of the story is, as La Fontaine's tale of the *The*

Tortoise and the Hare, which is to say take it slow and steady.

Also let us not confound speed with a rushed approach.

Fig. 9.-Blocking a left jab and countering with a left.

Fig. 10.- Evade a left straight punch to the right.

Closed guard.

When you want to fight in close, you should adopt what I will refer to as the closed guard, which is to say your left arm has a sharp bend to it and the elbow is placed up against your sides.

The arm describes a describes a come-and-go motion like a piston with limited range of motion.

The right arm which is still in the position indicated in the preceding paragraph is also drawn into the body.

Your head must be inclined with the chin almost touching your chest and your back is slightly bent.

This guard is called the crouch in America and England, while in France it is called the American guard. This is because many American boxers who prefer close-in fighting have adopted this style of guard.

Yet the boxer who displays the most perfect use of the crouch is the Englishman Johnny Hughes, a bantamweight fighter who came to France before he went to America.

Open Guard.

In the open guard the torso is held a bit more upright without raising up the chin.

The left arm is slightly bent and held more forward while moving forward and back somewhat.

You can hold the right hand a bit lower than you would in the closed guard, at about the level of the right nipple.

The right elbow must be placed a little below the right side.

Your feet can have less of a spread than was described above.

This guard is used for fighting at a distance.

From this position you can easily attack and stop the adversary with your left fist as well as firing counters with your right hand, above all if you have superior reach.

The figures above show the difference between the two guards, and these can be alternated over the course of a sparring session or a match according to need.

I cannot overemphasize the need to keep the legs long but relaxed rather than bent, above all in the case of the rear leg whichever guard you may be in, and the right shoulder must always be lower than the left (see figures 1 and 2).

How to hold your fists.

The fist is rolled by first bending the index finger, then the middle, the ring, and the pinky into the palm. The thumb is laid over the first two fingers, the index and the middle, resting on the second phalanges to be precise (see figure 3).

As you must strike with the flat of the fist which is formed by the first four phalanges, you must not bend the wrist as beginners often do (see figures 4 and 5).

The back of the hand follows the straight line of the forearm (see figure 4).

The fist must be placed in such a way that the fingernails are bottommost, or rather facing the ground (see figures 1 and 2).

How to move in boxing.

This is something you must work on the moment you come to stand in the guard, for it is of the utmost importance.

It is also easy enough for a child to do, and soon it will require minimal attention.

To advance.

You must move the left foot first while hardly taking it off of the ground.

As soon as the left foot is on the ground you can advance the right by dragging it somewhat. This is a natural movement without a "one, two" military tempo.

You can always advance slowly to avoid being surprised in the act by an attack which you cannot escape or block or evade despite all else because you lack stability.

You can easily understand that it is simpler to knock down a man in motion than a man who is immobile. Therefore keep in mind that you must advance cautiously and with balance.

(Fig. 11.[left]-Evade a left jab to the left, counter with a right to the body.)

To Withdraw.

(Fig. 12. [left]-Direct left to the body.)

First move the right foot back by lifting it ever so slightly, while the left foot follows dragging a bit in its turn along the mat. Whether you advance or withdraw your feet must remain at the same distance from one another and must never be brought together.

Advance and withdraw exercises must be worked very seriously, first without striking and then, when strikes have been learned, while delivering punches and counterpunches.

Here is an excellent progression to use in a lesson as soon as the student knows how to throw a left jab, a hook and a right uppercut. These three punches delivered to the face are ample for demonstrating a lesson in movement.

Advance.

1. First go slowly, breaking down the motions, then go quickly and smoothly.
2. Take several forward steps without pausing.

Withdraw.

3. Take a step back, breaking the motion down, then speeding up.
4. Take several steps back without pause.

5. Deliver a direct left jab after having advanced one pace, then after two, three, four, etc.

6. While withdrawing: Take a step back and stop the opponent's advance by throwing a left.

Repeat this exercise taking two, three, four, five steps back, etc.

7. Take a step back and throw a right hook.

8. Step back and deliver a right uppercut.

Repeat each of these exercises several times.

Once you know how to advance and withdraw, strike and advance then strike and withdraw. Learn to move to the side, which is very easy when the above motions have been mastered, as it follows the same principles.

If you move left, the left foot moves to the left first. If you move to the right the right foot moves to the right first.

Move aside when the opponent attacks, this is called a sidestep.

It is an easy evasion, but it must be quick and you must work at it often.

O must say that we see very few boxers, even champions, who do this correctly and, when it is done correctly and in context it is one of the sweetest moves in boxing.

I will have occasion to speak more of slips and side-steps further on in this book once the reader is more familiar with the techniques of boxing.

To finish with the question of how to move in boxing, I will give you this word of advice:

We see boxers moving continually and circling around one another. Now, whenever possible this circling should go to the right, and her is why: In moving to the right we put ourselves beyond the opponent's guard. While we move to the left we find ourselves faced with his hands and if he throws his right it has much more of a chance of landing, and with more force as we will be moving into it.

This blow will land with greater speed as we add our motion to that of the fist.

There is no rule without an exception however.

How and Where to strike.

Punches must be thrown with fists clenched to the body, face, sides and head (from the rules for English boxing for the French Boxing Federation). To throw useful punches it is important to strike quickly and with precision, seeking to impact the sensitive parts of the body and head.

First the fist must strike perpendicular to the body and return to its point of departure very quickly, rebounding as it were like a rubber ball.

Avoid striking the shoulders, forehead, or upper sides of the head, despite what the rules allow, for you risk injuring your hands, as the skull and arm-bones are harder than the bones of your hand.

The sensitive points to aim for are:

1. The body: The pit of the stomach, the lower ribs, the region of the liver, the left nipple under which the heart is located.

2. The head: The chin, the lower jaw, the nose and mouth. Of all of these the lower jaw and the tip of the shin especially can lead to the knockout, or at least put a man out of the fight.

A boxer is ruled out when he is sent to the mat and stays there for more than 10 seconds, or if he simply cannot fight for more than 0 seconds. The knockout is rarely dangerous. Most of the time it is occasioned by blows to the jaw as I have mentioned.

When a knockout is produced in this fashion a man is unconscious for a few seconds and feels no pain. He cannot even remember being hit. It is a sort of anesthesia produced by the jarring of the brain.

As for the knockout from a body-blow it is almost always produced by a strike to the solar-plexus where the sympathetic nervous system seems to be centered.

This kind of knockout is rather painful, as there is a feeling of suffocation accompanied by agony, but this only lasts for a few seconds.

Even a light hit to the chin can cause a knockout, while it takes a deal of force to knock a boxer out by striking him in the abdomen.

It is easy to harden oneself to the point where blows to the body do little harm.

The practice of contracting the stomach muscles in various ways on a daily basis can produce absolutely remarkable results, whereas any attempt to train oneself to endure direct punches to the face, especially to the chin, would be useless.

There are two very sensitive areas to keep in mind, though they are difficult to strike: the sides of the neck and the throat.

When a hard blow strikes one of these areas by chance the effect is always certain.

When you throw a bodyblow, as a general rule you should strike with a bent arm or "short" to use a term of art. In this way should the opponent manage to block with his arms, which happens often, the blow will not land on the low lines, since the tensed arm has become in a sense like a sword when it parrys.

How to protect yourself.

Block all punches to the face with your right hand which is held open in such a way as to catch incoming punches.

You must not think that the guard position alone is enough to keep incoming punches from finding their target.

You must in some way catch the enemy's punch in flight and close enough to your face where you will be ready to stop the next punch which will follow.

Sometimes you can block a left *swing* with your forearm.

This punch is frequent and powerful, and you will have ample opportunity to stop it in its course.

When the punches are blocked very close to your face or even against your face with only your hand intervening can they still be considered blocked?

Thus a parry or a block are the same thing, save that a parry applies more exactly when in stopping a punch thrown by the adversary be it high, low, or to the side, we find an sure means of firing a counter through a hole created in the opponent's guard.

Fig. 13.-Direct short left to the stomach & block.

Fig. 14.-Block a direct left & counter with a short left to the body.

Punches aimed at your stomach or the right side of your body are blocked by the elbow and the right forearm. Blows to the chest or your left side are blocked primarily with the back of the left hand held cupped.

Punches to the left side are blocked with the left forearm or elbow.

To easily block punches aimed at your face you must take care to keep your head down and offer a sort of head-butt to each incoming punch, as if you were giving each punch a nod.

In this way, if you miss the block the punch will impact your skull rather than sensitive points like the chin, nose, or mouth.

Now, as the skull is harder than the bones of the hand, you will feel little while the opponent who hits hard risks doing much more damage to his hand than he can inflict on your head.

If your opponent is wearing the 4 ounce gloves that are used in professional fights the case is much the same and you will not be at a disadvantage, as the blows will naturally land with less force.

This manner of receiving blows with the hard part of your head voluntarily is very practical and frees up one or both of your hands for more blocks.

To conclude this section on protecting yourself, let is be said that when you block a punch you should not seek to retain the hand but block it as abruptly as possible, just as with striking, and throw your counter right away.

The Classic Punches

Earlier in this book I said that you could become a decent boxer with month of lessons, regardless of your condition.

That may seem paradoxical, but it is easy to see the truth of what I assert when you consider that in "American" or "English" boxing (the nationality matters but little) there are but two punches, or rather two ways to deliver one punch.

I am speaking of the direct punch and the hook.

Some will say there are "swings" [haymakers] and uppercuts. But the "swing" is a wide hook and the uppercut is also a hook delivered from low to high. Thus the straight punch and the hook from left or right are the source of all of the others.

Here is why:

The left jab is delivered along a straight line like a fencing thrust. Just as with fencing, the strike is delivered with a lunging step forward. Of course the lunge is much less pronounced for a punch than for a sword thrust, and the arm does not travel so far. Indeed, in comparison it hardly moves at all.

Therefore the left jab, be it delivered to the face or body, always follows the same principle: There is a light quick step forward with the left foot which is set down with the heel hardly touching the floor at the same time the punch arrives at its destination.

This is what gives the punch its power.

When the punch is being thrown the right foot does not move.

When the punch is delivered from a distance to the opponent's face the arm is delivered without being loaded up and without quite coming to full extension.

At close range on the other hand you must load [coil] the arm up somewhat as this gives much more force to the punch.

To deliver a hook you don't need to step. The blow is delivered through a rotation of the shoulders.

The fastest and most effective hook is the right hook to the face or body. Naturally this is the first hook to learn after the jab and the cross since the right shoulder is held to the rear, which means that if you are in your guard or you have thrown a jab the power will come from bringing that right shoulder forward as you rotate your torso without having to move your feet.

The most favorable moment for delivering the left hook is naturally the moment after your have thrown the right hook.

Here is the maneuver:

The right fist strikes the face or body of the opponent, meaning the right shoulder is forward while the left must be back. As the right shoulder returns to its initial position, the left shoulder naturally comes forward and the left fist impacts the opponent's face or body with great force.

I will return to the execution of these punches in greater detail further on under their individual headings, and at the same time I will outline their blocks and appropriate counters.

The above description was merely meant to point out that there are really only two classic punches: Direct punches requiring a step, and hook punches, haymakers, and uppercuts which call for a rotation of the shoulders.

For those who are unacquainted with boxing and unfamiliar with the technical terms which serve to designate the different punches, I will give some explanation of the names which at times barbarous and at times creative. These comprise the language of pugilism.

A direct or straight punch indicates a strike delivered along a straight line.

A hook is thus named because the punch is delivered with a bent arm and not because, as some wrongly believe the punch itself describes a hook in space.

A cross is a counter-hook delivered in such a way that the arm crosses that of the adversary.

Oftentimes we hear the hook wrongly referred to as a cross.

Now, if a cross is always a hook, a hook is not always a cross.

The uppercut-- a difficult term to render in the French-- is a hook thrown low to high, generally under the chin when the opponent has a tendency lower his head or lean too far forward.

The swing is delivered in a wide loop.

The jab is a direct short punch delivered without much power.

The kidney punch is now illegal in France is of course a shot to the lower back.

A rarely used strike is the chopping blow. He we strike with the hand as if it were a knife.

Generally this strike is used when we are tied up body to body and the opponent has us by the belt.

When two boxers hold onto one another we say they are in a clinch. At this point the referee must separate them by saying "break away."

These various explanations being given, I urge you to work these punches until they are clean and effective in order to avoid messy boxing. You should strike almost at the same time as your opponent, using about the same amount of force he used against you.

I now pass on to a description of the main, truly useful punches in boxing.

Fig. 17.-Block a hook to the stomach.

Fig. 18.-Direct left to the face and block.

Extreme usefulness of the jab.

It is the main punch in boxing, the most useful, the easiest to deliver, and the one that poses the least risk in terms of your opponent being able to counter with a hard punch.

With the aid of the jab you can easily stop any attack.

When a boxer knows how to use his left jab, he can almost always beat men who are otherwise better than him from a strength and endurance point of view, but who have not mastered the use of this precious punch.

Certainly is is rare to see a boxer score a "knockout" with this punch, but on the other hand there is nothing more demoralizing than to have this punch coming at you constantly, and if it is too weak to put the opponent to sleep, it can be rather powerful when you strike repeatedly at the nose and mouth. Hitting someone repeatedly in these most sensitive parts of the face leave an impression, unless the man has a face of wood like the legendary invalid, hero of many fireside stories.

I know many boxers personally who manage to fare very well against champions because they make such great use of the jab.

I also know many a formidable boxer who have no fear of exchanging hooks and haymakers, but who will hesitate to step into the ring with a man of middling strength and endurance who is known for the use of his jab which is enough to stymie their furious onslaughts.

Obviously we cannot just use the left jab and a good right hook delivered at the right time and place often resolves the question of superiority.

But to land your right you must deliver it at the precise moment, while the left jab can be delivered at will.

Because of its utility and ease of execution, it can be extraordinary to watch beginners as they use it almost exclusively. It can also be comical to watch these same novices as they struggle to to throw their power-punch which will bring the knockout.

Needless to say a knockout almost never comes to crown their efforts, and if by some miracle they manage to pull it off it is often by sheer accident when the opponent more or less places his chin in front of the punch through carelessness.

So work on your jab, an excellent punch that consumes little energy and allows you to throw your hooks when the time is right.

At times you will see a double or triple jab. This usually means you have missed your first jab and with the second and third you find your range. Feel free to double up on your jabs, particularly to the face.

How to throw the jab.

While bringing your left foot forward for the step that accompanies the jab the arm begins to come forward on its course toward your opponent's face.

The fist must strike and rebound like a rubber ball to return to its point of departure the instant your left foot touches the ground.

If you wish to stay in place or fall back, the foot returns to its initial position.

If you wish to follow the opponent when he breaks off his attack, have your right foot come forward in the same manner as the left so as to maintain the distance between your feet.

When you take your step with the jab it should be about 20 to 30 cm. To make the punch more effective, constract the deltoid muscle which holds the arm to the shoulder. While delivering the punch incline your head forward somewhat to avoid a stopping-strike your adversary might deliver.

Avoid leaning forward too much, as a solid uppercut will remind you not to do so. While you throw your left your right hand opens to protect your face (see figure 8) and your right elbow covers your stomach.

Blocking the jab.

Block the jab to the face with your open hand, the back of the glove up against your cheek, while offering a little bit of counter-motion with your forearm (see figure 8).

Sometimes you can block with your forearm but while lifting the opponent's arm in such a way that you can throw a counter to your opponent's body more easily (see fig. 14).

The contrary block can be very effective (see figure 9).

Instead of blocking the incoming punch with an open hand you can strike him on the forearm near the elbow to unbalance him as he brings his weight forward, causing him to turn to the right.

When this block, which takes some skill, succeeds, it sets you up for for a left hook to the face or body. Your left passes under the opponent's left.

If you strike the face, your left passes over his.

Evasions and counters to the jab.

The easiest evasion is to slip to the right with a sudden advance. Your body and head lean to the right so that the punch passes over your left shoulder.

With this slip it is easy to throw a counter to the face with a straight left, the arm more or less bent depending upon the distance (see fig 10).

Thus it is the most favorable position to deliver a direct left to the stomach with your arm completely loaded up, the elbow squeezed against your left side (see fig 10).

Take care that when you throw a left counter to the body while evading you keep your right hand open in front of your face to avoid a strike from the outside of his right forearm delivered as he withdraws the arm.

When you slip to the left, again while lunging (see figure 11) the easiest counter is the right hook to the body.

The right arm actually comes to be trapped in some way beneath the left arm of the opponent who uncovers his left side by lifting his arm to strike.

You can counter with a right hook to the chin. You have to be quick about this.

If the opponent attacks with a straight left while keeping his head tucked, the easiest thing is to move left or right and deliver a right uppercut.

The right cross delivered while dodging to the left gives us the finest punch in boxing, but it is difficult to execute well. This is the right cross counter to the jaw.

It works like this: At the moment when the punch is thrown, incline your head to the left and hit him with a right hook above his left arm.

Your right fist must rise along a straight line passing along the inside of the hole formed by his deltoid and tricep (see figure 32). In this way the forearm is guided in some sense and the fist comes right to the chin. Take care to raise your right shoulder somewhat.

This "cross-counter" is more difficult to land on a boxer who keeps his chin up.

There is a trick one can practice to aid you in the cross-counter. At the moment when the fist lands, instead of withdrawing the arm to return to guard, lean your fist on the opponent's arm at the level of the shoulder to keep him from disengaging and throw a left hook to his stomach.

By drawing him to you with a tug the blow becomes more effective. Quite clearly this is done quickly so that the referee does not notice.

I have seen fighters who specialize in this move perform it so fast that the opponent does not know what is happening.

The use of such techniques is shady, and if I have illustrated it, it is above all so that potential victims know what is coming.

In dodging a left jab to to the face to the left you can also counter with a right hook to the chin inside the opponent's guard. The description of the right hook will be given later on.

Fig. 19.-Block a right hook with the left shoulder & hand.

Fig. 20.-Right uppercut.

A long jab to the body.

This is the same as the jab to the face, save that you must bend a little more to the right so that if the opponent blocks it you will be out of danger beneath his arm.

If he stops the punch with his right the blow will also be avoided since his right will pass over your back.

As a general rule do not use this punch unless the opponent is unbalanced to the rear with his hands raised to regain balance. It is an easy punch to block and often if the opponent blocks it with his forearm the punch can arrive too far below the belt.

In any case the punch has little effect unless it impacts the solar plexus or the pit of the stomach.

Block the straight left to the body.

Block this punch with your right elbow against your stomach.

You can also easily avoid it by fading back or pivoting to the right.

Some boxers are very adept at avoiding the straight body blow, bringing the stomach back with the left foot coming near the right.

It is, so to speak, a stomach dodge.

Short straight left to the body.

This is the best way to deliver a body-blow since the punch is delivered with a bent arm (see figure 18) and so has great force. Here the body weight comes into full effect.

To deliver the short straight left to the body you must take advantage of an attack wherein you make a feint to cause him to withdraw, or cause him to prepare a block. You move in right on top of him with a deeply lunging left foot. Your foot goes right under him between his feet.

At the same time the left foot touches the ground the left fist impacts its target, the arm coming from up against your body, the forearm arriving on the perpendicular is at a right angle to your upper arm.

Must also lean in with a little shove of the shoulder as you lean your body to the right so that if the opponent strikes with his left or right his strike goes too high.

This closing-in motion is one of the easiest counters to a right hook to the face, and I will speak of it again further on.

In any case it is one of the hardest body-blows and easy to deliver.

The fist should be turned so that the fingernails are almost facing the floor.

A good technique is to begin the strike with your nails facing you and rotate the hand at the moment of impact.

This is the famous *corkscrew punch* of Kid McCoy which he delivered with his right hook to the body.

Block the short straight left to the body.

Block the direct short left to the body with the right elbow placed in front of the stomach. You can also block it by bringing the left glove to the right elbow, resting the hand upon the elbow with the palm turned toward you.

This is actually a great way to block.

From this position your body and face are covered, the right hand protects the face and stands ready to deliver a counter in the form of a hook to the jaw should the opponent not take the precaution of leaning to the left when he strikes.

Countering the short straight left to the body.

Earlier I explained and demonstrated this block and how you can reply with your right hook to the jaw.

You can also reply with a left hook to the jaw. In blocking with the right elbow you can turn your body a bit to the left bringing the left shoulder back ready to come forward to deliver the left hook.

If the opponent does not rise up quickly enough after getting low for the short straight left to the body, a left uppercut or a right to the chin is possible.

In the case where you counter with a right uppercut, be sure to take the time to turn your body a bit to the left when striking to reach your opponent more easily.

The ultimate goal is to land your punch at the very moment he lowers his stance so that your rising uppercut meets his falling jaw.

This is puts an end to many a boxing match.

Hooks

As I have already pointed out, hooks are punches thrown with the arm bent.

When you throw a direct punch the power comes from the small step forward which recruits your body weight, while with a hook the power comes from the rotation of your shoulders.

Now if you shoulders make a semicircular motion the forearm moves along a straight line perpendicular to the target without moving the upper arm.

Fig. 21.-Block a right uppercut

Fig. 22.-Left uppercut & quash the left hook.

Of course I am speaking here of classic punches that are easy to execute, the fastest, most effective, and least likely to be blocked.

Clearly a boxer who throws a punch with a bent arm, even a haymaker, is throwing a hook, but there are hooks and then there are hooks.

A haymaker is a wild hook thrown by someone who has never learned to box or who has learned poorly.

The hook I have in mind is after the model of Frank Erne and Willie Lewis, specialists, if there is such a thing, in this classic punch.

Most of the knockouts they scored against many unfortunate opponents were owed to this famous punch which, with their consummate knowledge of boxing, brought them much justified glory.

It this is just what is lacking among English boxers, though marvellous at working the left, which they land so to speak at will, aided by their great footwork which is the hallmark of their style.

All of those who have had the chance to watch them fight in Paris have seen them deliver their hooks with their arms bent in haymaker style. For this reason they find themselves pound for pound at a disadvantage to French fighters who have instinctively seized upon the style of their American brothers-in-arms.

It is much harder to adjust a haymaker than a hook. Moreover it is much easier to see the haymaker than the straight punch.

In the beginning young boxers who are not flexible by nature find it rather hard to twist their bodies in order to throw a proper hook.

I would recommend that beginners exercise with lateral twists of the torso, first with hands on hips and then with arms extended.

These two exercises must be done daily for about a minute to begin, and over time they should be increased incrementally to five minutes.

These movements are executed at a rate of about a second per twist with the feet placed about 40 cm apart.

The trunk must turn at the pelvis, which is to say the legs should not be involved, remaining immobile as the lower back increases in flexibility.

Right hook to the face.

(see figure 15.)

From correct guard position you should bring the left shoulder and arm back with the fist coming to be placed at the left nipple.

At the same time this motion brings the right shoulder forward. The upper arm remains in line with the body while the forearm moves along a straight line directly toward the opponent's chin.

As soon as the punch is thrown, whether it lands or not, you must return to guard with the right shoulder drawn back as if by a spring.

By all of this I mean that the whole motion is of a piece and we do not count *one* for the outgoing punch and *two* for the return of the arm.

Strange to say that the power of the punch comes from the swift withdrawal of the left shoulder rather than a pushing of the right shoulder and arm.

The right arm does not move except that the forearm directs the fist to the target.

This punch does not require strength but skill, timing, and quickness without hurry.

(Left: Fig 23.- The "swing" or haymaker)

To deliver the hook properly you must incline the left shoulder a bit such that the right shoulder is even with the opponent's chin. Your head should lean to the left and a bit forward to avoid a possible counter. This way the counter will land on your skull which is not sensitive.

Your feet must not move if you are returning a punch or if you find yourself in close.

(Left: Fig. 24.-Block the "swing" with the side of your hand.)

If you make a feint in preparation for an attack, you must bring your left foot forward and a bit to the left (this brings your foot between his). The foot touches down softly just a moment before your punch lands. If you hit him right on the chin a knockout is certain.

This punch must be delivered with skill, the fist tightening just at the moment of impact. Therein lies the majority of your effort.

Block the right hook to the face.

Block with the palm or hollow of your right hand placed against your chin. Some boxers block with the left hand backed up to the side of the head. This is less effective and more dangerous, as it exposes the left side of the body. If the punch is not hard, or if you are tightly guarding yourself, use your skull to block. People may laugh, but let me explain. You won't be blocking with your nose or chin, but with your forehead and above, and the bone here is harder than the bones of the hand. When boxing with 4 ounce gloves, even with padding, there is a chance for the opponent to hurt his hand, and after that his right will be less dangerous, as he won't want to make the same mistake twice.

I have often heard disgruntled boxers use the excuse that they hurt their hands with a punch. From my point of view, this is no excuse but proof of their poor technique-- or the superior technique of their opponent.

Your hands will be safer if you take care to wrap them properly in linen and take care to strike soft targets. I imagine that ancient pugilists were well aware of this phenomenon as they began their sport bare-handed. I suspect this is likely what led to the used of the leather straps. These were not so much offensive instruments as a means of protecting the hands that they were sure to break even when hitting the soft targets like the nose and face.

They made use of the leather to bandage their hands in the same way modern boxers wrap their hands in cloth.

Without a doubt many fighter used the skull to stop hard punches. In this case simple leather would not be enough to protect damaged hands which could not longer inflict much damage on the opponent. This likely gave rise to the method of loading the leather with bits of lead in order to be able to inflict some damage.

And indeed the very use of lead as opposed to other metals seems to support my idea, as other metals would have been to hard and caused too many skull fractures, whereas lead would flatten against the cranial bones.

I came to believe this by examining Greek statues and sketches. I was struck by the fact that their guard position was just like that of modern boxers employing the "crouch" or "American" guard.

They had the same manner if inclining the head hand keeping their arms bent and close to the body. There really is nothing new under the sun! We were not the first to see the superiority of methods we consider modern, even though they date back several thousand years.

Excuse this long digression which interrupted our demonstration of the punching techniques and blocks of boxing.

Evade the right hook to the face.

The slips you can use include dodging straight to the right placing yourself against the opponent's left side with your left foot between his legs, a rotational slip which was described earlier, and fading back with the upper body. It is easy to evade a punch by side stepping to the left (see figure 40).

Countering the right hook.

The easiest counter is the block counter, which consists in blocking the incoming punch with your right hand while turning your body a bit to the right so that the left shoulder comes forward to aid the right hand in blocking. Return a right hook immediately.

It is in order to avoid this counter that I mentioned returning to your guard quickly in the section on the right hook.

If your opponent neglects to do this you will land your punch for sure.

You can also throw your counter to his body but this will take more time.

Another excellent technique is to fade back with the upper body, then throw a counter as you come forward without even a tenth of a second's pause.

Counter with your left.

Throw your left jab right away. Slip left and get beneath your opponent's right hook and fire a short left to his stomach, stepping deep into his stance with your left foot right under him to unbalance him (see figure 18).

Same-time counters.

If he aims at your face, get low with your head forward and a bit to the left, bringing your left foot forward and to the left so that you find yourself outside of his right arm.

At the same time fire a hook at his chin by passing your arm beneath his (see figure 33).

This counter is formidable and few of those who are caught by it can get up within the required 10 seconds. The contrary movement of the opponent doubles the force of the blow, and the adversary is in bad position.

A counter to the stomach is just as easy since the opponent finds himself well out of guard position with his body exposed (see figure 30).

Right hook to the body.

The right hook to the body is aimed at the breadbasket toward the left side or the heart as an attack or as a counter to a left. If he throws a right you can throw a right hook to his liver which is on the right side of the body.

In striking and attacking you should step forward with your left while twisting your body as if to deliver the same strike to the face, but you must place your forearm at the level of his midsection.

Keep your upper arm against your body to support it and return immediately to guard, retracting the left foot to its original position, though not too rapidly.

Before delivering this punch you can feign a left to the face by stretching your arm out toward the opponent. When you then retract the left arm to the rear you lend it more power, above all when you leave no pause between the motions.

When you are close in with the opponent there is no need to step forward, and you deliver the hook to the body with your feet planted.

Block the right hook to the body.

(See figure 17.)

I can think of only one really effective block against a right to the body. This is to block with your right elbow against your breadbasket with your open left hand touching the right elbow. Your right hand remains up by your chin with the left shoulder helping it to protect you.

The right straight to the face.

This is not my favorite punch since it leaves you wide open, though it is well used by many boxers.

Fig. 25.-Block the "swing" with your forearm, left jab.

Fig. 26.- Left "swing" to the body.

To deliver the right straight punch you proceed in exactly the same way as for the right hook save that you straighten the arm which increases the power of the punch.

Blocking the straight right.

Blocks for the straight right are the same as those for the right hook. There is yet another I would add since it is excellent though hard to master.

It contains both a slip and a sidestep.

When the opponent throws his punch, take your sidestep to the left and somewhat forward while blocking with your left hand on your arm at chin level. To achieve this block you must bear in mind that as you take your step to the left you must turn your body somewhat to the right, arching your back to entirely remove your head from the path of the punch. When the shoulder and the right arm arm drawn back you are ready to throw your counter of a right hook to the face or body which will have great power (see figure 40).

To practice this block and counter, break it down into two parts:

1st take the step to the left while blocking with your left hand and prepare your counter by loading up your bent right arm.

2nd deliver the counter of a right hook by withdrawing the left shoulder and arm quickly.

The right arm passes under the opponent's arm whether you hit his head or body.

This same block and counter can be used for a right hook as well as a right straight.

An excellent counter to use is the left cross while leaning your head somewhat to the right to slip the right straight punch.

Left hook to the face & body.

It seems reasonable to call the left hook a short left jab as well since it is delivered with the arm bent as in a hook. But what I term a hook in particular is the punch delivered with the rotation of the shoulders. The force of the jab comes from the step that accompanies it.

The best exercise to give a student is to have him learn to deliver the left hook after a right hook once this latter punch has been mastered.

Here we can take advantage from the rebounding of the right fist as it returns from the opponent's block to bring the left fist forward to strike the opponent's face or body. We can deliver the left hook as our lead punch as well.

To do this we strike while advancing the bent left arm following a slight and quick withdrawal of the left shoulder. This movement is all of a single piece, while at the same time the right hand is held forward to block the incoming left.

As a counter the left hook must be thrown to the face or body while the right arm comes out to parry a left straight punch thrown by the opponent (see parries/blocks for the straight left).

Blocking the left hook to the face.

When the punch comes in to the left side of your face when you find yourself on the same line as the opponent you should block with a short sharp knife-hand strike to the opponent's right wrist.

You can then profit from this position with his right on the interior line of your guard to transform your parry into a right hook to his jaw or chin by making your right fist slip along the left arm of the opponent.

It is easy to stop the opponent at a distance with a direct left to the face.

Fig. 27.-Blocking a left *swing* to the body.

Fig. 28.-Fade back.

Slips & counters to the left hook to the face.

Slipping to the right, pass your head beneath the attacking arm and counter with a straight left to the breadbasket.

You can also evade by fading back. Come forward again and counter as the opponent returns to guard.

The twisting slip is also easy, and you can use it to fire a left hook to the opponent's stomach.

Counters to the stomach are easy when the opponent must lift his left arm to deliver a hook, thus uncovering his whole torso.

Block the left hook to the body.

Just like blocking a short straight punch to the stomach.

Block with your right elbow, leaving the right fist primed to counter with a hook.

The right uppercut.

Use the right uppercut against an opponent who comes in with his head low, or at the moment he slips a left. It is easy to deliver a right uppercut after feigning a left, which can lead the opponent to avoid the punch he thinks he sees coming.

Execute the uppercut with the right fist like a hook, but the punch moves from low to high with the forearm passing along the opponent's chest.

As with the right hook it is the same manner of drawing the left shoulder and arm back. Try to hit the chin which is most sensitive.

In a *clinch* or when close in it is a very useful punch. To place it for certain effect you must be inside of the opponent's guard. Then slide your forearm up the opponent's thorax like a piston.

This is the best punch for *in-fighting* or close quarters, and it works beautifully when fighting against amateurs who don't know how to slip properly.

The left uppercut.

The left uppercut is used against an opponent who slips down to your left when close in. Throw the punch while hoisting your left shoulder up.

Block the uppercut.

Block the uppercut by placing your open right hand in front of your face with the palm turned out so that the back of your glove forms a cushion that considerably deadens the blow.

Countering the uppercut.

You can fake a slip so that the opponent goes for an uppercut, at which point you can throw a *swing* or a straight left which won't be blocked since the opponent's right arm is throwing an uppercut.

The left *swing* to the face.

I'm not a great fan of the *swing* as I prefer straight punches which are quicker and harder to evade. Moreover it requires great skill to deliver a swing with precision.

Beginners should avoid this punch given the difficulty of execution. But of course, this is the opposite of what happens. It seems easy to the beginner to swoop his arm like a windmill.

You will see men who don't know how to box use this punch in the street. They trade wild haymakers by turns trying to connect with *swings.* They are sloppy haymakers but swings nonetheless.

To throw a correct swing with your left, let it fall and then rise again as it describes an outside semicircle at the level of the opponent's chin. Turn your shoulders from left to right and lean on your right shoulder at the moment of impact. The left foot pivots on the toes with the heel coming to the outside.

You should turn the fingernails out somewhat while bending the wrist back a bit to strike with the knuckles where the phalanges join the metacarpals which are the bones that form the bulk of the hand. If you don't turn the fist out you risk striking with the thumb, a common injury in street brawls.

Fig. 29.-Rotational slip for a *swing* to the face.

Fig. 30.-Slip the right hook & counter with a left to the liver.

Parry the left "swing" to the face.

Block the left swing with a right knife-hand or forearm parry (see figure 24).

Some prefer the forearm block, but it does uncover the your right side and stomach.

Slipping the left "swing" to the face.

The best and easiest slip is directly to the left, then come in for the clinch. You can also fade back from the punch. Skilled boxers also make use of the rotational slip.

Counters to the left "swing" to the face.

When you execute the first parry, reply with a direct left stopping punch or counter with a swing to his face or body. With the second parry, you can use the same swings or a straight left to the stomach. You can also counter with a right hook to the chin or side. This latter punch, whether you have blocked or slipped to the left, should be thrown immediately while stepping into the opponent.

With the rotational slip, the best counter is the left hook to the breadbasket.

The left "swing" to the body.

This is delivered to the opponent's right side when he holds his arm too high in the guard, uncovering the area above the belt-line (see figure 26).

To the deliver this punch draw the shoulder and fist back a little to bring them forward with a whipping motion. Hold your fist as you would for a swing to the face and pivot a bit on the toes of your left foot, turning the heel out.

When throwing the swing, never straighten your arm out completely.

Blocking the left "swing" to the body.

This is easy using the right elbow. Place your open right hand to the left side of your chin, as very often a right hook will follow a left swing (see figure 26).

The right "swing" to the face.

This is best used when you have the opponent on the ropes. You can use this violent punch for the *knockout.*

From guard let your right fist fall, then raise it to the level of the opponent's jaw describing a semicircle which moves on the horizontal plane until the fist hits the target. Pivot on the right toes with your heel turning outward. The left foot stays in place.

Blocking the right "swing."

The best block is with your forearm against the opponent's wrist.

Slipping the right "swing."

The opponent is wide open due to the excessive movement of the right arm, and it should be easy to land a right hook to his jaw. This is the classic counter.

The right hook to the stomach can also be used from a rotational slip.

After blocking with your left arm you can counter by coming back in with a right hook to his jaw or stomach.

If you evade the punch by backing up, come back in forcefully with a straight left to his face above his outstretched right.

Footwork.

A real boxer must be able to move around the ring with the light step of a dancer, all while observing the principles laid out in the chapter on movement.

It takes time, of course, to acquire good footwork, and you must be gifted with dexterity to be able to roll with the punches.

Skipping rope is the best way to get good results toward this end.

At the end of three or four months of skipping rope your results should already be appreciable, provided you work the exercise almost daily for fifteen minutes or so.

At first five or six minutes are enough, then you must work your way up progressively.

Do not overdo this exercise, as it is very taxing on the heart.

You should jump from your toes starting with your feet close together, then change to alternating the feet, first staying in place and then moving forward, back, right and left.

At the end of four or five weeks you will arrive at a great level of skill in this exercise which at first glance seems like a game for little girls. In fact it is a marvelous tool for physical conditioning.

There is nothing like it for developing the abdominal muscles and of course the legs.

As you develop dexterity and quickness in the legs you must exercise your augmented power of motion while boxing, but only when called for and while maintaining the necessary distance. Don't give yourself over to jumping all around in the name of fancy footwork and keep yourself too far from the adversary.

Footwork has one goal: to keep you out of easy range at exactly the right distance so that unforeseen attacks are avoided, all while allowing you to reach the opponent with ease at the right moment.

Secondly, the leg muscles have to work hard to sustain the shock of attacks and counterattacks. After each engagement you ought to make three or four little bobs from on leg to the other as if performing a little gymnastic move while keeping the legs long and supple.

This relaxes this muscles in an incredible way.

To do this little dance you must withdraw and bring your feet relatively close together, then return to guard right away with your feet far enough apart to maintain good balance.

With the help of good footwork your advance, retreat, and side to side motion will become lightning fast which becomes effortless.

Perfect your footwork, which is to boxing what strategy is to war. Indeed, Napoleon was fond of saying that he won his battles with the legs of his soldiers.

It was in fact the incredible rapidity of his marches and counter-marches that disoriented the enemy and allowed the great general to attack like lightning at precisely the points where the foe was weakest at the very moment when the enemy thought him out of striking distance.

It is the same with boxing. We advance when the time is right to put the enemy in a corner or on the ropes, or we break off to draw an attack which will open the way to a deadly counterattack.

All of it is subordinated to the well developed instinct for what needs to be done at a given moment, which is the boxer's greatest guide.

Fig. 31.-Left cross counter to a right straight.

Fig. 32.-Right straight counter to a left jab.

Combinations.

Once a student perfects the individual punches in the repertoire-- which is not difficult since these consist of the straight punch, the hook, the swing and the uppercut delivered with the left or right hand to the head or the body-- he begins to throw combinations with his left and right, never losing contact with the opponent.

This work has already begun when the student works at twisting the torso to throw hooks. I need not go into the twisting action of the shoulders again.

What is important is the way in which combinations are put together and executed.

One could say that a guiding principle is to always change the order of punches. Thus a punch to the face should be followed by a body blow and vice versa.

I will make an exception for the first series of lefts and rights which must be delivered to the face and then to the body. Since we first learn to deliver one punch, it is only logical that our first combinations should consist of two punches. Below I shall provide a sort of ladder with which to progress through combinations. I have experimented with such exercises through the course of my teaching career and have achieved remarkable results.

Such exercises can be performed with the instructor or with a punching bag, a big leather sack stuffed with cotton rags.

One rule that should never be discarded is that of lowering the head and to a lesser extent the body away from the punching arm. If you punch with the left lean right, and if you punch with the right lean left. This will keep you in perfect balance on your legs.

Ladder of Combinations: 2 punches.

1. Left jab and right hook to the face.
2. Right hook and left hook to the face.
3. Left jab to the face and right hook to the body.
4. Right hook to the face and left hook to the body.

5. Left jab to the body and right hook to the face.
6. Right hook to the body and left hook to the face.
7. Left jab to the face and right uppercut.
8. Right uppercut and left hook to the face.
9. Left jab to the body and right uppercut.
10. Right uppercut and left hook to the body.
11. Left uppercut, right uppercut.
12. Right uppercut, left uppercut.
13. Right hook and left uppercut.

Combinations: 3 punches.

1. Left, right, left to the face.
2. Left right to the face, left to the body.
3. Left to the face, left right to the body.

4. Left to the face, right to the body, left to the face.

5. Left to the body, right left to the face.

6. Left right to the body, left to the face.

7. Left to the body, right to the face, left to the body.

8. Left, right , left to the body.

9. Right, left, right to the face.

10. Right left to the face, right to the body.

11. Right to the face, left right to the body.

12. Right to the face, left to the body, right to the face.

13. Right left right to the body.

14. Right left to the body, right to the face.

15. Right to the body, left right to the face.

16. Right to the body, left to the face, right to the body.

You can throw in some uppercuts to add to these combinations which I shall add to perhaps without reason in order to give you a proper sense of the underlying concept.

Working from the above outline it is easy to progress to four punch combinations. Of course it is not necessary to work through each and every one of these combinations when you train, as this would demand too much time and energy. Keep in mind that every punch should be delivered for maximum power. These exercises are superb for those looking to build up their stamina and endurance.

PRACTICING SLIPS.

A slip allows us to avoid punches aimed at the face by moving the head off of the line of attack. A good slip is performed with as little movement as possible, and we remain as close as we can to the opponent's fist to be sure we are set up for our counter.

Each time we slip we should counter right away, for that is the goal of the move: The opponent is missing an arm with which to block, and we still have both hands with which to hit him.

Never hesitate but never slip prematurely either. Remember that he might be faking a punch, and then you're in trouble since you've been drawn out of good position and into bad.

These are two kinds of slips, the direct slips which bring the body back or to the sides, and the rotational slip.

DIRECT SLIP.

The direct slip is used for all straight punches (left or right) to the face. These are simple and easy to do and will put you out of the enemy's line of fire. For an incoming left slip left of right, it does not matter, though the right is preferable.

At the moment the opponent strikes, advance and lean the head, and to a lesser extent the body to the right (see figure 10).

The incoming fist then passes over your right shoulder, and you should throw a stopping punch, a left jab, to his face or body.

To slip left you must also go forward while leaning the head and body slightly left.

When slipping to the left of an incoming left, the easiest counters are the right hook to the body or jaw and the right cross to the jaw.

Counters are always delivered with the opposite arm to the incoming punch. Thus when you slip left counter with your right hand and when you slip right counter with your left.

FADING BACK.

This move is also simple and very useful when facing an opponent who does not punch scientifically, but instead makes use of big haymakers in a fight (see figure 28).

You can also avoid straight punches by leaning back in this way.

The name of the move more or less describes it. When the punch comes in lean back and let it pass, then lean in with your counterpunch. It is easy to see the danger of leaning back for too long, however. You would then find it difficult to evade a renewed attack.

Fade back without moving your feet, or you can bring your right foot back or somewhat to the right.

If you counter after a fade take care to lean to the side opposite you striking hand and pass under your opponent's attack arm.

ROTATIONAL SLIP.

This one is hard, and you have to have a certain talent to use it, a certain suppleness, dexterity, and skill to be able to pull it off in the classic fashion.

Moreover it seems almost impossible to teach this slip with written words and a photo, as these will not be able to impart a real comprehension. That said, I'll give it a try (fig. 29).

When the punch comes in you should slip forward into the opponent's guard and move your head to the other side of the punching arm by passing underneath it. The head describes a semicircle with the opponent's arm as its center. All of this is done with great speed.

If the punch is a "swing" or haymaker you just lower the head and raise it when the arm passes. Start by leaning the head *with* the incoming strike. Thus for a left haymaker lean your head *away from* the punch, get low, then rise up after it has passed. For a right "swing" lean your head to your right, again *away* from the punch.

Admittedly this is hard, but there's nothing prettier than a well executed series of rotational slips.

Fig. 35.-Side-step left, load up the right counterpunch.

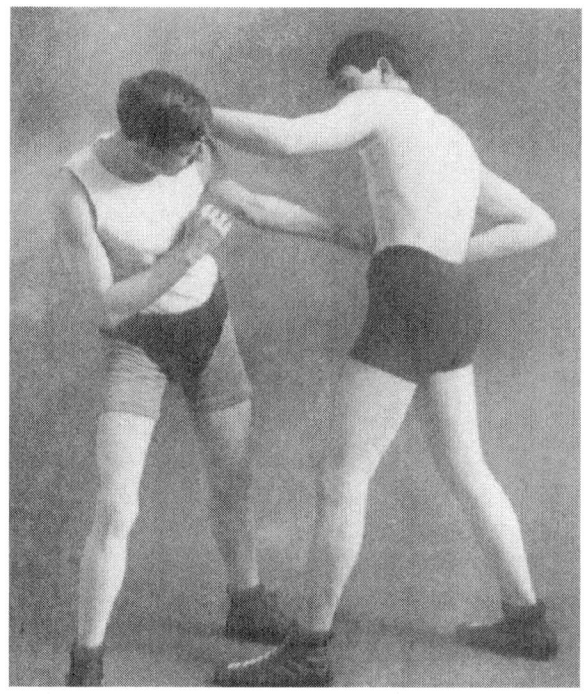

Fig. 36.-Side-step right & left to the stomach.

THE CROSS.

I have already explained the cross which is, as it were, a hook delivered while crossing the enemy's punch. The use of the cross is greatest when the enemy throws a straight left. The left cross is only used for the right straight punch. It is harder to throw than the right cross both for subtlety and the fact that for most the left hand is the off hand.

LEFT CROSS.

If the opponent comes in with his right straight, throw a left stopping punch and step forward while leaning right. Instead of throwing your stop punch inside of the opponent's guard, load the arm up enough and pass it over the incoming arm. For better effect, follow up with a right hook to the stomach.

This second punch should be easy since the opponent has uncovered his body by turning left (see figure 34).

RIGHT CROSS.

Slip left to avoid a left jab to your face while delivering a right hook to the jaw, passing your arm above the opponent's without lifting your elbow to the outside.

Make your fist pass through the opening formed by the opponent's arm between the bicep and shoulder, striking his chin. It is up to you whether you step in to deliver the right cross, and it is difficult to deliver a clean shot to the chin is the opponent keeps his head down.

BLOCK THE RIGHT CROSS.

To avoid eating the right cross, the best thing to do is to keep your head down while throwing your left jab. Keep your chin in tight to your neck and your left shoulder high to protect your jaw on the left side.

To be really cautious, keep your right hand up against you chin with the palm facing out while your right elbow protects your breadbasket to block the inevitable left jab, as this is the perfect partner to the right cross to the jaw.

SIDE-STEP

To avoid a frontal attack and gain some room to work on your counter, take a step to the right or left.

TO THE RIGHT.

Most often a left jab should accompany your step to the right. You could also step left with this jab but you risk eating a right by opening yourself up. As the sidestep is meant to create space, I would say you should avoid a left step with a left jab. To step right, move the right foot laterally some 40 cm.

If you want to strike in close with some hooks, the left foot must stay put. But is you wish to continue the fight at a distance the left foot must follow the right so that you find yourself entirely outside of the opponent's line. Your opponent will often become unbalanced when suddenly there is no one in front of him. You can exploit this by throwing a punch, often a very effective one, whether it be a straight left, an uppercut, or a right hook to the body.

STEP TO THE LEFT.

This can be useful when facing an opponent who strikes from a distance with wide hooks or right straight punches.

The left side-step consists in placing your left foot laterally to the outside to the distance of about 40 cm at the very moment your opponent comes in to throw his right. Keep your right foot planted.

At the same time, deliver a right to his face or breadbasket which will be wide open.

FEINTS.

Feints fool the adversary and are followed with a quick attack along another line.

Pretend to throw your left to lead your opponent to throw either a stopping punch or any other while you step in to get good range. You can also where his tender spots are as he moves to block a phantom punch which he sees as being aimed toward a particular part of his body.

The most common fake is the head fake rather than feigning a punch of some kind. Menace him with your left hand aimed at his face. Step in with your left foot and out again immediately, bending your head in and then drawing it back as if to offer a target and then retract it.

This should be done continually to exhaust the other fighter and keep him guessing, making him easier to hit.

Another excellent feint is the fade, such that when you see the opponent prepare an attack you pull away and to the right.

Another good feint is the right sidestep. Put your foot to the right and bring it back immediately to strike your enemy in a surprise attack.

GENERAL SPARRING TACTICS (RINGSMANSHIP).

Many boxers owe the majority of their wins to their knowledge of ring-tactics or "working the ring."

This knowledge is indeed important in determining who will win a fight. For this reason a fellow with the greatest physical and mental abilities will lose to a less gifted man who knows how to work the ring, at least the first time around.

The situations and positions in the ring through the course of a match are so diverse that it takes a long time to experiment and come to know them so that you can make a good showing.

Fig. 37.- Side-step right & counter the left jab.

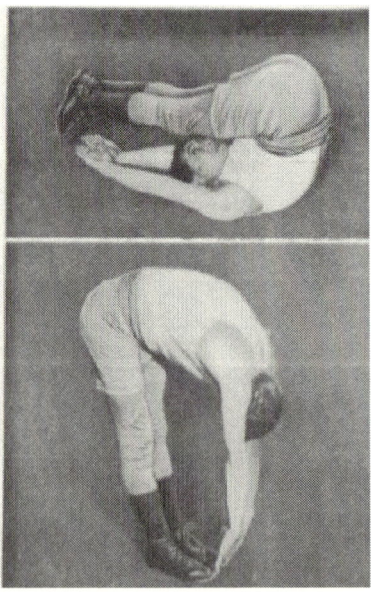

Fig. 38 & 39.- Stretching. Flex the torso standing & laying down.
Develop the stomach muscles to protect yourself from punches.

That said, there are a few tricks and rules that it is very good to keep in mind.

Rounds are of 2, 3, or 4 minutes in duration and are separated by a minute long rest period. In France professional fights have 6 to 20 rounds of three minutes in length separated by a one minute rest. In England amateur championships have 3 rounds of 2 to 3 minutes in length, with a final 4 minute round.

Professional fights have 6 to 20 rounds of 2 or 3 minutes. 3 minute rounds are reserved for the big matches, especially those in which the championship is being disputed.

The signal to begin or end a round comes from a gong, bell, or whistle, or at times an official will simply shout *time!*

At this the fighters, who have been sitting in their corners, get up and approach one another and put out their hands to touch gloves, especially at the beginning of the first round of the match. There is a traditional shaking of hands at the end for the sake of courtesy.

There are times when fighters will forego good manner and approach the opponent without extending a hand, trying to make the other fellow look a fool for coming out with his hand stretched forth, and even using the occasion to get a punch in on the exposed opponent.

Such regrettable instances happen all to often, and a sucker punch like this can sometimes tip the balance of the fight in favor of the ill-mannered fighter. It has now become the standard, especially in championship bouts, for the fighters to shake hands, be it upon entering the ring or when the referee has brought them together in center-ring.

In such instances it is agreed that the fighters will not shake hands upon the commencement of the first round.

Referees should also be aware that at times the final handshake becomes the occasion for a disgruntled fighter to sucker-punch his opponent.

STUDY HIS GAME.

When facing off with another boxer you must study his game intently insofar as possible, making several feints to different areas to find the points he means to protect the best and how his various defenses make openings in his guard. If he guards his stomach and sides heavily he has no faith in them, and so you must attack them at all costs.

If it is he jaw he protects most zealously it means he can't take blows to the head. At the same time you must determine the maximum range of his best punches. As this distance is essentially fixed you must then seek to stay just beyond his range.

Put yourself beyond his ideal range by a few centimeters, or even just inside of his ideal range if you find that from there you can strike effectively.

In moving try to keep to the center of the ring and put your opponent on the ropes or in the corner.

When cornered, for this is a critical position seeing as you cannot move back, right or left, you must move left when he throws a right and vice versa. The best way out of a corner is step into the opponent with a series of jabs.

Once you get the hang of this it is easy to escape from the corner by forcing the opponent to cover up.

Always be decisive in your attacks and never hesitate or be timid. Never stop with your feints. Fake moving in and out and come back with combinations delivered with energy. Keep menacing his face with your left.

Never lead with your right hand, but always lead in with a left jab or a feigned left jab. With the fake jab, bring your glove as close to his face as possible. Only use your right hand when your range is proper. A right thrown from outside rarely reaches its target.

If your opponent comes in with both guns blazing in an impetuous manner, it is easy to stop him with some left jabs to the face, particularly if you have superior reach. If he comes in with greater fury still with his right, strike his right as he withdraws it.

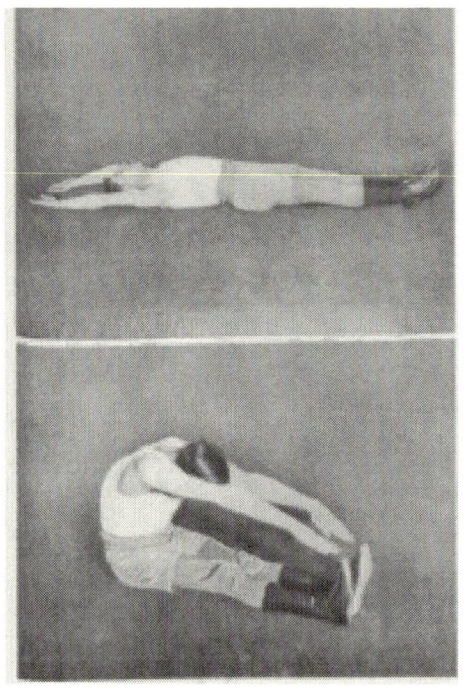

Fig. 40 & 41.-Stretching

Fig. 42.-Working the bag.

If on the other hand your opponent has greater reach who works with long-range jabs, your easiest response is to throw stopping punches to his body.

Always meet a punch with a counter and don't think one of his punches doesn't count because it doesn't hurt. Give as good as you get regardless.

Try to throw punches that at the very least will score points with the judges.

If your opponent has size and reach advantage and it is hard to get at him, turn every engagement into a bout of "infighting" and avoid being kept there.

If your opponent is smaller and the match is long, bodyblows are best for exhausting the other man and making him retreat as he gradually gasses out.

Never forget that once your body-blows cause him to drop his hands you should throw a punch to his now-exposed face.

If you bring the opponent down to the mat with a punch to the jaw and he rises before being counted out, hit him in the stomach. If he was knocked down by a body-blow, swing for his head.

Once a boxer is hurt he covers the affected area more than before. A man who takes a really good shot to the stomach will reveal his jaw without fail.

Be sure to throw a right every time he does. When he throws a left use a left stopping punch or counter, or throw a right counter-cross to his jaw or stomach.

For every right hand he throws you should throw a right hand. If he throws a left throw a stopping punch with your left or even a right cross to his face or body.

If you send him to the mat remain three or four paces away from him and wait for him to return to a full stand before attacking. Return to the attack at once without rushing, first to be courteous and second to get a sense of the opponent's state. It often comes to pass that a desperate opponent throws a wild punch that lands easily because you are thinking only of finishing your opponent off and not of defending yourself.

These are even boxers who pretend to be more hurt than they actually are, and when their opponent enters in on them with a mind to finish them, they suddenly come alive and try to throw that one killer punch on their unwary opponent.

Avoid talking during a fight as much as possible and never address the judges or the referee in a loud voice. Never show discontent or object to a poor decision. Doing so is futile and the decision of the ref and the judges cannot be changed in any event.

SUMMING UP.

Take care to:

Lace your gloves correctly.

Make sure the soles of your shoes have a decent amount of resin on them.

See that your belt is done up right.

Rinse your mouth with water before boxing.

Never mock your opponent.

Never respond to the audience.

Be respectful to the ref and the judges.

Never show contempt for your opponent no matter how feeble he may be.

Follow your coach's instructions, as he can see what is occurring from outside the ring.

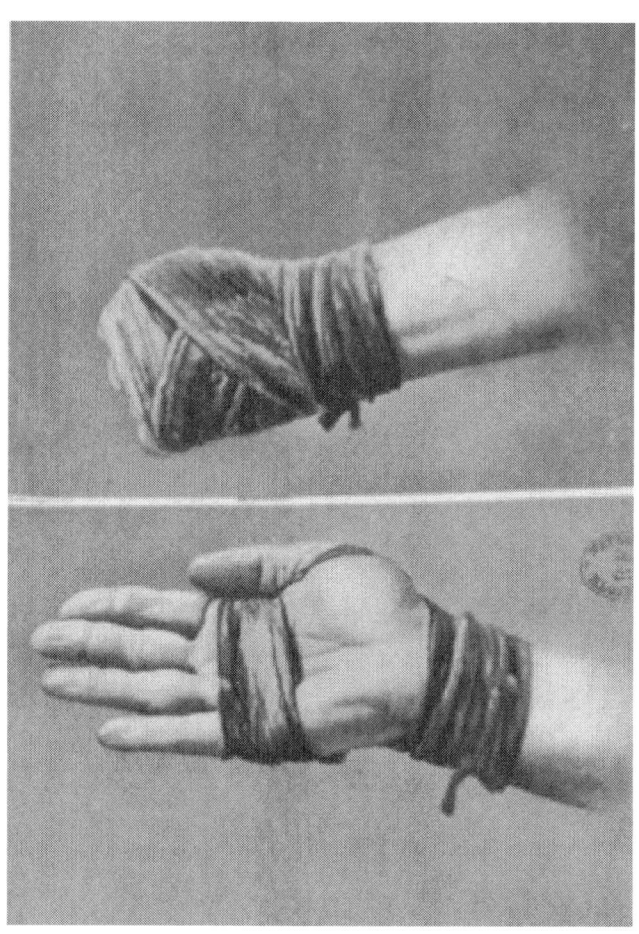

Fig. 43.-Wrapping the hands.

Fig. 44.-Ear protection for training.

Avoid shaking hands save when it is necessary, for there are boxers who, after delivering a foul punch or even after a clinch, will try to make things right with an excess of courtesy. Be courteous, but never appear weak.

TRAINING.

Faced with a match of any kind, championship or otherwise, a boxer must train. This means daily practice of relevant exercises directly related to boxing for a determined period of time according to the difficulty and duration of the match. In this way the boxer is in the necessary shape in terms of mental and physical conditioning, power and endurance.

The duration of a given exercise and the overall training period varies somewhat according to the boxer's temperament.

The mark of a good manager is to know how best to dose out a man's training to fit his needs.

Here are some exercises you can use:

First you must walk every morning in the country or in a park. This is called *footing.*

It works like this:

After breakfast you should put on several sweaters and several pairs of socks, then dress up in some warm pants. Throw on a warm hat and a heavy scarf. In winter you should wear a woolen gloves. Get a good pair of light shoes.

You don't need to dress like this in the summer. In Europe the mornings aren't hot, and if you have weight to lose and want to sweat, cover yourself in order to add some heat, even in the summer.

In winter you should hit the road as soon as it gets light, and in warm weather by six in the morning, but never by later than seven.

ROADWORK.

According to the strength and temperament of the fighter, the distance to travel varies from 8 to 10 km, or even more than 12.

It is excessive to force a man to run further than this, save in exceptional circumstances.

When it is time to work out is best to find a road or field at random. There are great cross-country routes where you can find slopes, stairs, ledges, and all manner of obstacles.

Have the boxer walk for 1,500 to 2,000 meters, then sprint for 100 meters, then walk again for the same distance as before, then run for 400 meters and so forth until the training period is done.

It is good to throw in some sudden sprints of 30 to 40 meters, and then some backwards runs of 60 to 80 meters.

Immediately after your workout take a quick shower of 5 or 6 seconds followed by a rub with rough linen or a horsehair glove. Change clothes and underclothes.

Roadwork should last for from an hour and a half to two hours. After this rest until lunch.

WORK IN THE GYM.

After lunch take a short walk to aid in digestion. Begin work at the gym two and one half to three hours after eating, when digestion is complete and you can resume work.

Start with some light stretching such as flexing the arms with or without deep breathing exercises. Stretch the torso by bending forward and back, first with your hands on your hips and then with them stretched out. These motions are performed while standing.

Strengthen the abdominal starting from a supine position. Raise your straightened legs in unison and then let them down slowly until the heels touch the floor. Now do one leg at a time.

Gather your bent legs into your stomach and then stretch them out with the toes pointed. First do this with both legs and then with one leg at a time.

Still in the supine position, spread your legs and raise them up, then lower them slowly so that your legs come down to the ground spread wide. Now join them and repeat the motion three times more.

Stretch your arms out above your head. Bring your legs in and your arms up so that your hands meet your feet. Now come slowly back. Now lift your torso and arms only until you can touch your feet before returning to the start position slowly.

Stand up and raise yourself up on your toes, first with your feet together and then with your feet some 40 cm apart-- these are two different exercises.

From standing, raise your straightened leg out in front of you, then the other. Now raise each leg to the side in turn.

Raise a leg to the rear while balancing on the toes of the other foot. Execute these movements ten or twelve times. As with stretching, I recommend the types of lessons set down in a book by lieutenant Hebert, of which there are 12 different series. The exercises I have just described are drawn straight from this book which can be found in any store.

Still, beyond all of these wonderful exercises I would recommend jumping rope, which should always round out all other exercises. First keep your feet together, then jump with alternating feet. In a short time you will become very dextrous, and you will be able to build on your rope-skipping regimen.

I know some boxers whose rope-skipping routines are worth paying admission to see.

This exercise should last from 6 to 20 minutes.

PUNCHING BALL & BAG.

A punching ball is an egg shaped sphere hung by a cord or a leather strap beneath a hardwood platform. The platform is affixed to a wall or a stanchion of the sort used for pull-up bars.

It is placed at a sufficient height to be accessible without being able to strike the puncher in his face. There are various kinds of punching balls with different mounts to be found at every sporting-equipment shop.

The punching ball exercise is excellent for hand-eye coordination, speed, and precision.

It is absolutely essential for a pro boxer to exercise with a punching ball for 15 to 20 minutes each day. Some fighters become so skilled with this work that their routine could become an act at a music hall.

A rational training method consists in allowing the fighter to work the ball at will for a while to get used to it before having him treat it as an opponent, feinting, practicing footwork, and throwing combinations while moving forward and back.

Finish the session with a few really hard punches thrown with the feet planted.

Fig. 45.-A good *1-2 punch.* The left leaves as the right arrives.

Fig. 46.-The left in a *1-2 punch*.

Be sure to recruit the shoulders into the motion of the punches. After the punching ball you must work the punching bag to develop power and stamina, and above all to harden up your hands and wrists.

The punching bag is a sac made from canvas or leather and filled with cotton rags.

Don't fill the bag with sand or sawdust, etc. Sand is too hard and heavy. I've seen fighters hurt themselves terribly on sand filled bags, and sawdust produces far too much dust.

You can find cotton rags at any cloth merchant's shop. They're used for cleaning machinery. The dimensions of the bag should be 35 to 40 cm diameter and 60 to 80 cm long. Hang the bag from the ceiling with a rope and pulley so that the bag can be raised and lowered at will. The heavy bag is great for combination drills.

You should really hit the bag with 4, 6, or 8 ounce gloves according to the gloves that you'll be wearing in your next match. You must also work the bag with bare fists and regular gloves.

Practicing with gloves gives you better precision, for if you practice without gloves you will find yourself a bit off when it is time to wear them for the match. On the other hand you should learn to box with bare hands for the sake of self defense. I have in fact known boxers who have always worn gloves and who have found themselves less able to deliver a proper punch bare-fisted.

The best way to work the heavy bag is to go at it for 2 to 3 minute rounds with 1 minute of rest in between, just as if you were in a match.

Two to four rounds are sufficient for a good session.

SHADOW BOXING.

A good training exercise is shadow boxing, which means as you might think, to box with your shadow. The boxer goes at it with an imaginary opponent throwing punches and parries in the air.

Don't punch with power but work your slips hard. Again, 2 to 4 rounds of 2 to 3 minutes are enough.

SPARRING.

Naturally the best workout for a boxer is to box. This seems too obvious to mention and yet it is too often neglected by those who believe that all you need to win a match is sufficient stamina.

If you are feeling worn down or a bit under the weather, you should feel free to shave off every other part of your training regimen *except* for sparring. Always follow a progression of 2 to 3 rounds at the beginning of your training period, and when you have reached peak conditioning go to 5 or 6 rounds.

Once or twice a week you can go up to ten rounds, but never more than this. In general you should decrease the number of sparring rounds in the week before the fight in order to avoid fatigue.

A boxer should spar with several partners so he can learn to work with different styles. Never spar too hard to avoid going into your match with a sprained hand, a black eye or a broken nose. Wrap your hands well with some 5 cm wide strips of Velpeau cloth. This cloth is available at every pharmacy.

Don't bother with the gauze called "Chatterton" as it offers little protection.

Most hands require one roll of Velpeau, big hands require one and a half. Never cross the wrap on the inside of the hand but always on the back (see figure 43).

For a match you can add 1 meter 50 of Chatterton on top of the Velpeau wrap for best adherence. In this case powder your hands well with talc once they are wrapped so that you can get your gloves on and off with ease without messing up the wrap.

For training you ought to wear some kind of ear protection. There is a sort of open headgear you can wear with an elastic band under the chin that allows your ears to be protected by sponge pads which will absorb hard blows and keep you from developing what boxers call "cauliflower ear." I have noticed that these types of injuries happen mostly on training, and while they are not dangerous they can be rather painful.

WORK THE CLINCH.

You must know how to hand the jostling action that occurs within the clinch. The two fighters will grab one another by the nape of the neck or the shoulders and push or pull trying to unbalance one another.

As the only result they seek a result relevant to boxing and not to bring the other fighter to the ground, they use only the force needed to push or pull the other fellow forward or back somewhat. It is a good exercise in terms of stamina and development of the lower back and legs. You can practice your clinch-work after sparring or before. I prefer after, as working the clinch can be tiring.

MASSAGE & SHOWER.

Massage is great when performed by a professional for 45 minutes or at least a half hour. Otherwise it will be incomplete and the result will be almost nil as a result. In such a case it would be better to replace massage with a rubdown with a horsehair glove or some rough cloth.

Massages and rubdowns must be preceded by a cold or tepid shower. A cold shower should last from 12 to 14 seconds, and should be avoided after exercise unless you have broken a sweat. This is an important point.

REGIMEN.

Any boxer who is undertaking serious training must follow a certain nutritional program during his training period in addition to his severe physical and psychological preparations.

First off, his diet ought to be as diverse as possible without surpassing the set caloric limit. You must eat abundantly, but not to excess.

Always finish eating with a bit of room left in your stomach. Eat red roasted or grilled meats accompanied by green vegetables. To work on your stamina you should avoid bread, potatoes, and grains in general. In the winter above all you should eat some peas, beans, and lentils.

If you can't give up bread, try eating some toast instead. Some toasted bread about the size of your hand with each meal is excellent.

Delicate stomachs will want to avoid raw vegetables and salads seasoned with vinegar. As a general rule raw vegetables should be avoided in the week prior to a match.

From time to time you should switch from red meats like mutton or beef to lamb and chicken. Avoid heavy sauces like red and white sauces. Undercooked or raw eggs are without equal.

A bit of fresh butter, some jam, and rice pudding are great.

As for beverages, drink as you always do though in a lesser quantity with meals. Avoid full-strength wine, save for half of a glass at the end of a meal. Avoid fermented foods like strong cheese as well.

Fresh cheeses like white cheese, Gervais, and Pommel are preferable.

Avoid stews and soups.

Below you will find a model menu which can be modified according to circumstances.

Breakfast.

Soft-boiled or raw eggs.
Toast with butter or jam.
A cup of tea or coffee with milk.

Lunch.

Steak or cutlet, grilled.
Green vegetables: cabbage, green beans.

White cheese, cream cheese.

Dessert.

Fresh fruit or rice pudding.

A slice of toast.

Half & half wine, water.

A finger's width of bordeaux.

Dinner.

Roast beef and vegetables or peas and lentils.

Toast.

Cheese & dessert.

Same as lunch.

You can drink between meals, just not alcohol. You should take a 30 to 45 minute walk after each meal. Never smoke. Try to sleep 10 hours a day and get up at 6:00 am, 7:00 am at the latest. An athlete in training needs at least 8 hours of sleep. Show reserve in your dealings with the fair sex.

Breaking the above rules can cause you to lose the

Fig. 49.-Backfist to the jaw. Illegal without gloves, but allowed with gloves or when delivered to the stomach in the manner shown above.

Fig. 50.-Kidney punch in the clinch.

the fruits of several weeks of training.

Between each match your should allow yourself a week or two of rest.

Take advantage of down time to eat some of the foods forbidden during your training regimen. Strictly avoid alcohol and tobacco.

If your rest goes beyond a week, you should still do some light training in the gym three or four times a week to avoid getting rusty. This happens faster than one might think.

During training you should set aside a full day for rest-- Sunday for example and a half day on Thursday unless you have weight to lose. Stop training at most 2 days before your match at most, and at least take the evening off before your fight, depending upon your constitution.

You should lighten your workload for the week preceding a fight. If the match is at night, stay in bed longer than usual on the day of the fight so that you aren't sleepy at the time of the fight after having developed the habit of turning in early.

It is great to train outdoors, but is the fight is to take place in a closed hall, you must work inside during the week before the match in order to become used to the feeling and not make a sudden switch.

Advice to corner-men.

Here is what you must do if you are charged with caring for a boxer.

Arrive early at the place where the match is set so you can prepare your man for the fight at leisure and without haste. This keeps him from becoming fatigued.

Have some laughs with your fighter and never leave him alone. Make it clear that he is the certain victor in this fight.

Make sure to have a bucket of cool fresh water. Throw some slices of orange in there and, if available, some ice.

The water will serve to wash and refresh the boxer during his fight.

To rinse the fighter's mouth prepare a bottle or pitcher of water with lemon juice or mint as an astringent.

Get yourself a big sponge and some smelling salts for your man to sniff if he grows woozy or gets hit hard.

Put all of these things in the charge of someone you trust. Be sure the boxer wants for nothing.

Be sure his belt is neither too tight nor too loose. Make sure his shoes are laced up correctly. A boxer should not wear brand new shoes to a match. Always use the well worn shoes from training to be sure your man is at ease. Massage the boxer or have someone else massage him for a sufficient time.

Have him rest under a cover on a cot or a table with his head somewhat elevated. Bandage his hands carefully and have everything you need for bandaging at the ready.

Ringside.

Be sure there is no puddled water in your corner. If there is some sponge it up and wash the area somewhat with water from your bucket and a little resin. Be sure you have enough resin and that the bucket you use for dirty water gets emptied.

Only use materials you have prepared personally in the locker room.

Clearly define a task for each corner-man. Two men can be in charge of towels, a man below the ring can stand ready with utensils, and the chief corner-man can give the boxer water to drink and sponge him. Another man can warm and massage the boxer's legs.

Only one man advises the boxer, since when several men speak at once you risk confusing the fighter with contrary counsel.

A few seconds before time is called at the end of each round the caretakers must be ready to jump up and get to work. As soon as the end of the round is signaled a corner-man places a stool up in the corner of the ring.

Make sure to fan some air at the boxer's face and not his knees or stomach, as fresh air is essential.

Don't offer your advice in a loud voice, but by signs to avoid being overheard by the opponent, who will then know what to expect from your fighter.

Only give advice at critical moments.

During the match, never let your man put his arms down so that he is open to the opponent. Two things must always be kept in mind:

Keep your head down and your fists up.

I have noticed that it is almost always when a man lifts his chin and lowers his hands that the lucky punch comes in unforeseen.

During breaks remind your man that he is going to win, but that he must move faster to be sure of clear win if he does not have the advantage.

Be sure to wash your fighter down at every break.

There are other tricks and tips that one acquires through experience, but the main thing to remember is that a good corner-man can be the architect of victory.

Fig. 51.-Kidney punches are legal from a distance.

Fig. 52.-Illegal strike with the palm.

Boxing Rules of the French Boxing Federation.

THE RING.

The ring shall have the following dimensions: 7 meters maximum to 4 meters minimum per side.

The platform must be solid and well made, extending beyond the ropes by .5 meters on each side. The floor shall be covered with strong, tightly stretched canvas, under which there shall be a layer of felt to deaden the shock of falls.

The ring shall be surrounded by three strong hempen ropes that are at least 2 cm in diameter and covered in cloth. They should be stretched tight and well maintained on four or eight round wooden posts, from 1 meter 30 in height above the level of the ring and padded on those parts facing the ring. The posts can also be outside of the ring. The ropes shall be spaced at .6 meters, .9 meters, and 1.2 meters from the floor of the ring.

ATTIRE.

Decent attire shall be worn with light, unpointed shoes, with new gloves of good quality.

GLOVE WEIGHT.

For professionals of all classes, the minimum weight for each glove shall be 0.114 grams (4 ounces), and the maximum weight shall be 0,228 grams (8 ounces).

For amateurs in light weight categories the gloves shall be 0.171 grams (6 ounces), and for those in middle to heavyweight categories gloves shall be at least 0.228 grams (8 ounces).

WEIGHT CLASS.

Minimum weight to 46 kilos.

Fly weight to 50.8 kilos

Rooster weight to 53.32 kilos

Feather weight to 57.15 kilos

Light weight to 61.23 kilos

Middle middle weight to 66.68 kilos

Middle weight to 72.57 kilos

Middle heavyweight to 79.38 kilos.

Heavyweight, no limit.

Weight is determined by a scale when the boxer is disrobed. Weigh in occurs at the regulation time which must be in the evening on the day of the fight.

CORNERS.

Amateurs are allowed one corner-man and a helper to help during rest periods.

The corner-man and his aid have no right to enter the ring before the signal for the end of a round, and they must leave the ring with their equipment when told to do so by the timekeeper 10 seconds before the fight recommences.

It is strictly forbidden for corner men to signal to or instruct their boxer during a round.

All infractions will result in a penalty.

If a corner-man tries to aid in helping a fallen boxer to rise by sprinkling him for water for example, and the boxer is helped by this maneuver, he is immediately disqualified. The boxer is not penalized if the help in ineffective.

ROUND DURATION.

For amateur championships, each match will have 4 rounds of 3 minutes each separated by a rest of 1 minute.

For professionals the number of rounds varies according to conventions and the length of rounds can be 2 to 3 minutes each, but always separated by a 1 minute rest.

A signal given by the timekeeper announces the beginning of the round, and the boxers immediately quit their corners and fight. When the signal comes to end the round they must break off immediately and return to their corners.

A timekeeper is charged with keeping time for:

1. Overall time
2. Round length
3. Rests
4. Stoppages

DECISION.

Fights, matches, and championships are controlled by a single referee, up to 3 judges and a director.

The referee or the director comes into the ring with the purpose of instructing fighters to abide by the rules.

ONE REFEREE.

In the case of a single referee, he will make decisions in all cases and proclaim the result in a decision which cannot be appealed.

3 JUDGES & A DIRECTOR.

When a fight director is aided by 3 judges he has the power to decide a fight in the following cases:

1. If a serious foul is committed such that it ruins a fighter's chance at the win, he can disqualify the perpetrator immediately.
2. In cases where one fighter is manifestly inferior to the point of being in danger the director can stop the fight and hand the win to the stronger opponent.
3. In the case of doubtful fouls that do not hinder the affected boxer's ability to fight, the director

can issue a warning to the perpetrator and, after issuing three such warnings, he can disqualify the guilty boxer on the fourth.
4. The director can separate clinces, count a man out when he goes down, and when he reaches 10 the adversary is declared the victor.

LOW BLOWS.

In doubtful cases where the director has not seen a foul clearly though the "victim" appears to suffer, or pretends to suffer, the director looks to the judges. If, as is usually the case, the judges have seen the low blow, the perpetrator must be disqualified. If the judges have not seen the low blow, the fight is stopped and the victim is examined by the ringside physician. If the doctor determines that there was a real injury, the perpetrator is disqualified. If not, the boxer pretending to be hurt can be disqualified.

The director does not decide fights that go the distance, he can only be consulted. The final awarding of points is left to the 3 judges alone.

When the 3 judges agree, the boxer with the most points is declared the winner. When there is disagreement among the judges and a clear majority cannot be determined the match is declared a tie.

AWARDING POINTS.

When there is no knockout victory is given to the fighter who, according to general opinion, has shown himself superior, keeping the following things in mind:

1. Attacks delivered with both hands.
2. Defense.
3. General knowledge.

4. Punching power.

5. Endurance.

KNOCKOUT.

In the case when a fighter falls to the mat the referee begins counting to 10 immediately in a loud voice so as to be heard, insofar as possible, by the fallen man. This 1 to 10 count is delivered with a second between each number, but the total time should not exceed ten seconds.

The referee or director must rely upon the timekeeper who, watching all of this, begins to mark time visibly the moment a man goes down.

Whenever a fighter cannot rise after 10 seconds a knockout is pronounced by the referee. If the round is over before the man is counted out, he is saved by the bell.

When a fighter is down, the other boxer maintains his distance and the referee or director keeps himself between the fallen man and his opponent. When the fallen man rises they can begin boxing once again.

DEFINITION OF FALLEN.

For a man to be down, his knee at least must be touching the mat.

DOUBLE KNOCKOUT.

In case of a double knockout, the boxer with the most points wins.

REGULAR PUNCHES.

A regular punch must be delivered with a closed fist above the belt to the face and the head.

ILLEGAL PUNCHES.

It is illegal to punch below the belt, to strike with an open hand, with the palm, the wrist, the forearm, the elbow, the knife-hand, or to strike while pivoting to the rear. It is illegal to strike a man on the ground, to grab the opponent, to kick, deliver head or shoulder strikes, wrestle, shove an opponent against the ropes, or hit him in the kidneys during a clinch.

CLINCHING.

It is only a clinch when both men are grabbing one another. So long as a man isn't clinching, which is to say has both hands free, he can continue to fight. A boxer who grabs a man with one arm cannot strike with the other. In any case the command "break" means both men must release one another and take a step back, then resume boxing.

CALL TO ORDER.

For minor and unintentional fouls that do not put anyone at a disadvantage, the referee will issue a warning to the offender. All such calls to order must be announced so that the public can hear the nature of the foul committed. If the same infraction or two more different infractions are committed by the same boxer, the fouls will all have been announced publicly, and the offender will be disqualified without recourse upon the fourth infraction. Observations may be offered to the fighters by the ref without rising to the level of calls to order.

BANDAGES.

Bandages will be provided by the fight organizer and will be provided in equal amounts to both boxers.

NO CONTEST.

No contest is a term applying to both boxers in a match. The penalty amounts to forfeiture of the fight and the fight contract. This decision is only announced when it seems clear that the two boxers are in connivance and are not defending themselves to the full extent of their abilities. Such a ruling is considered a sanction and not an indication that match never occured.

THROW IN THE SPONGE.

Only the corner-man recognized by the boxer himself has the right to throw in the sponge in recognition of his fighter's defeat. This must be recognized and accepted by the parties involved before a new round begins or it will not be recognized.

INCIDENTAL REASONS TO STOP THE MATCH.

When gloves, shoes, or trunks come undone the referee or director must see that these are put back in place immediately, and the timekeeper will keep track of the interval.

If by some strange chance gloves of the right weight cannot be found in the whole establishment, the fight will be stopped and moved to the soonest possible future date. If possible the referee and judges should be the same. The same rules apply to some act of God, be it the police, a riot, or a fire.

A decision like this is not recorded, and it is as if the match never took place.

ACCIDENTS IN A FIGHT.

If a boxer is wounded to the point where he cannot continue or he falls out of the ring and cannot get back in within the stipulated ten seconds, he is declared beaten.

SIMULATING THE KNOCKOUT.

Any boxer who pretends to be knocked out voluntarily without being hit with sufficient force is considered knocked out after ten seconds, but this has no bearing on whether the federation will level fines against him.

RULES FOR BOXING IN THE NATIONAL SPORTING CLUB OF LONDON.

MATCHES.

1. All matches will be fought in a ring surrounded by ropes and measuring not less than 14 feet per side and not more than 20 feet per side.
2. All fighters will wear light shoes or slippers, Gloves will be of 6 ounces in weight or more. Fighters will undergo a physical examination

prior to entering the ring and will be weighed on the day of the match. Bandages will be examined and measured and left with officials on the day the contract is signed. The bandage for each hand will be no more than 6 feet long by 1 inch wide.

3. For each match the number of rounds must be specified. No match may exceed 15 rounds except for championship bouts which must not exceed 20 rounds. Rounds will not exceed 3 minutes and rests will last for 1 minute.

4. Boxers are allowed to have two corner-men whose names will be submitted to the approval of the committee. Corner-men must leave the ring when "time" is called, and they will not offer advice or assistance during a round.

5. A timekeeper and a referee will be designated by the committee for each match. The referee

can accord no more than 5 points to the better man at the end of each round and a proportional number to the other man. If he finds them to be equal both are given 5 points. If a boxer falls he must rise within the 10 seconds allotted without help. The opponent is kept away from him during this time and boxing only resumes when the referee say so. If while rising the boxer touches the ground with any part of his body, even if one or both feet are on the ground, he is still counted as being down. A boxer who cannot continue to fight after 10 seconds gets no points for rising and the fight is ended. The referee confers victory on the fighter with the greatest number of points. If at the end of a round one boxer has so many points that the other man cannot possibility catch up to him or beat him, the first boxer is declared the winner. Points are awarded for: attacks, punches that land fully with the part of the glove protecting the knuckles connecting with the face, the side of the head, or the body above the belt. Points are also given for defense, guard, footwork, slips and evasions. In cases where points are equal victory is given to the man who dominated the fight or who showed superior style.

6. The referee can disqualify a boxer for any of the following reasons: shots below the belt, pivot punches, kidney punches, open hand strikes, and wrist or elbow strikes. Grabbing, head-butting, shoulder strikes, intentionally falling without getting hit, wrestling, brutality, or any other illegal move can lead to disqualification. The referee can stop the fight if one of the

competitors is clearly outclasses or somehow becomes incapable of defending himself.
7. If the referee believes a man has intentionally thrown an illegal strike, the boxer can be stripped of any prize.
8. All infractions by a boxer and his corner can lead to disqualification.
9. In cases not covered by these rules, or in cases where rules are open to interpretation, the referee will make the final decision.

BRITISH CHAMPIONSHIPS

Regulation weights.

Flyweight-8 stone (50.8 kg)

Bantam weight-8 stone 6 lbs (53.52 kg)

Featherweight-9 stone (57.15 kg)

Lightweight-9 stone 9 lbs (61.23 kg)

Welterweight-10 stone 7 lbs (66.68 kg)

Middleweight-11 stone 6 lbs (72.57 kg)

Light Heavyweight- 12 stone 7 lbs (79.38 kg)

Heavyweight- all weights.

Weigh-in takes place 8 hours before the match.

Every boxer must defend his title of British Champion within 6 months after gaining his title for a stake of at least 100 pounds sterling (2,500 francs) except for heavyweights whose minimum is fixed at 200 pounds sterling (5,000 francs) and flyweights whose minimum is set at 50 pounds sterling (1,250 francs).

A challenge must be accompanied by a deposit of 50 pounds sterling in order to receive the approbation of the Committee of the National Sporting Club.

Belt challenges will be attributed to these championships and must be maintained for a period of three uninterrupted years or be won through three consecutive fights in order to become the definitive property of the belt-holder.

It is not allowed for a belt-holder to defend his belt in any weight class save the one he gained it in order to keep it. Should he lose he must relinquish his belt.

Made in United States
Orlando, FL
02 May 2025